Oral Poetry in Africa:
the Abagusii of Kenya

Christopher Okemwa

Copyright © 2021 Christopher Okemwa
All rights reserved.

This publication may not be reproduced, in whole or in part, by any means including photocopying or any information storage or retrieval system, without the specific and prior written permission of the publisher.

This book is sold subject to the condition that it shall not, by way of trade or otherwise, be re-sold, hired out, or otherwise circulated without the author's or publisher's prior consent in any form of binding or cover other than that in which it is published and without a similar condition including this condition being imposed on the subsequent purchaser.

First Edition: January 2021

Published by Nsemia Inc. Publishers (www.nsemia.com)

Editor: Matunda Nyanchama
Cover Concept: Author
Illustration: Robert Maina Kambo
Cover Design: Linda Kiboma
Layout Design: Bethsheba Nyabuto

Note for Librarians:
A cataloguing record for this book is available from Library and Archives Canada.

ISBN: 978-1-989928-04-2

Acknowledgements

A piece of work like this cannot be the result of the efforts of an individual. Many people provided perspectives, ideas and input (actual poetry & even vocalizing the same) that went a long way to shaping this publication.

This work was originally conceived as part of a three-part volume that I termed the *Oral Literature of Abagusii*. The three components were oral poetry (this volume), riddles (published as *Riddles of Abagusii of Kenya* (Nsemia Inc. 2011) and proverbs (published as *Proverbs of Abagusii of Kenya: Application and Meaning* (Nsemia Inc 2012). I am grateful to professors Kefa Otiso and Justus Ogembo along with Dr. Matunda Nyanchama, my publisher, who counseled reconsideration of the approach. This resulted in the production of the three parts separately. That technique was fortuitous as it allowed me more time to focus on and enhance the oral poetry and context presented in this book while the other two works were already available for readers.

As I developed this work, I collected input and interpretation from a number of people. These pieces appear in this work, making it richer than it was initially envisioned.

Many thanks go to Ms. Monica Nchore Okiamba who sung to me most of the poetry in this collection. I received poems from a number of people, including Mr. Timothy Nyarera Ongubo, Dr. Evans Omosa Nyamwaka, Mr. Sam Keganda, Ms. Christine Bundi, Mr. Obino Nyambane and Dr. Matunda Nyanchama. I offer abundant appreciation to them.

Prof. John S. Akama offered and contextualized poems pertaining to war and rites of passage. The late Julius Nyakwama offered a version of the latter that further illuminated and enriched this important landmark in the journey of people born in Gusii. I am greatly indebted to them.

Mr. Nemwel Mogere Atemba contributed, sang and contextualized poetry relating to marriage, weddings and nuptials. I owe him a ton of gratitude.

Very special thanks go to Mzee Samuel Beda Ombasa Tamaro for offering, vocalizing and contextualizing more than 21 *emeino* (Abagusii classical Songs) in this collection. Mzee Tamaro's deep understanding of Gusii culture and history is matched by few others within and outside the community.

Dr. Felix Orina Oyioka generously permitted me to use materials from his Ph.D. Thesis while Mr. Abai Ochoi's book *The History and Traditions of the Abagusii of Kenya Mwanyagetinge* (2015) proved to be an invaluable resource. To the two, I say thank you and urge that they continue researching and writing some more.

The same applies to the late Nelson King'oina Nyang'era and his book *The Making of Man and Woman under Customary Laws* (1999), which was vital in contextualizing many Abagusii cultural practices to which the poetry pertains.

Jane Obuchi not only permitted us to use some of the poems in her collection titled *Chingero chi'Abagusii* (2019), but also read the entire book with a toothcomb. Her input and corrections were invaluable.

Space does not allow me to list everyone who contributed to the successful compilation of this book. Likely, you offered me an idea, a suggestion or perspective that went into influencing the way this work turned out. For your effort and contribution, I am indebted to you even when I have not mentioned your name.

Let me also thank my publisher, Nsemia Inc. Publishers, for staying with me throughout this time I have been working on this project. I hope that your patience, taxing as it may have been, was worth it.

Finally, I thank my wife and children for their patience with me while working on this project. I realize what the long absences from home, while I was in the field, meant to you. However, as they say, nothing good comes without sacrifice. I am eternally grateful that you continue to make sacrifices even as I pursue such scholarly endeavours.

Table of Contents

About the Author vii
Preface xiii
Emeino - (Classical Lyrics of the Abagusii) xvi
Chapter 1
Chapter 2 - Poetry for Children 5
Chapter 3 - Poetry for Circumcision Ceremonies 21
Chapter 4 - Poetry for Marriage Ceremonies 43
    Before Courtship 43
    Poetry of Courtship 57
Chapter 5 - Oral Poetry during Marriage Ceremonies 69
Chapter 6 - Poetry for Married Men and Women 83
Chapter 7 - Poetry of Old Age 97
Chapter 8 - Poetry During Death 101
Chapter 9 - Poetry of Inter-clan Skirmishes, Inter-Ethnic
    Wars, Cattle Rustling and Praise for Animals 103
Chapter 10 - Poetry of Historical Events, Immigration and
    Settlement 139
Chapter 11 - Poetry Sung During Work 143
Chapter 12 - From Tradition to Modern 149
Summary, Conclusion & Recommendations 159
Glossary of Terms 163
References 165

About the Author

Christopher Okemwa is a lecturer of Literature at Kisii University, Kenya. He is the founder and director of Kistrech International Poetry Festival in Kenya.

His poetry collections include: *The Gong* (Nsemia Inc., 2010), *Purgatorius Ignis* (Translated to French; Nsemia Inc., 2016), *Ominous Clouds* (Translated to Norwegian, Finnish & Greek; Nsemia Inc., 2018); *The Pieta* (Translated to Armenian, Պիետա; Narcis, 2019), and *A Withering Rose* (Translated to Polish and Bohemian Vadnoucí růže; 2019). He has also published a short story collection, *Chubot, the Cursed One and Other Stories* (Nsemia Inc., 2011). His published collection also includes three children's books: *The Visitor at the Gate*, *Let us Keep Tiger* and *The Village Queen* (Paulines Africa, 2010, 2011, 2013). This is in addition to four oral literature works, *Riddles of the Abagusii People of Kenya: Gems of Wisdom from the African Continent* (Nsemia Inc., 2011), *The Proverbs of the Abagusii of Kenya: Meaning & Application* (Nsemia Inc., 2012) and *Otenyo the Great Warrior of the Abagusii People of Kenya* (Nsemia Inc., 2016).

Okemwa has written five folktales of the Abagusii people of Kenya in *Ekegusii* language: *Ogasusu na Oganchogu* (The Hare and the Elephant), *Ogasusu na Okanyambu* (The Hare and the Chameleon), *Ogasusu na Okanyang'au* (The Hare and the Hyena), *Okang'ombe, Okanyang'au na Ogakondo* (The Cow, the Hyena & the Monkey), and *Kerangeti na Kerantina* (Kerangeti and Kerantina).

Okemwa's novella, *Sabina and the Mystery of the Ogre*, won the 2015 Canadian Burt Award for African Literature (Kenya). Its sequel, *Sabina the Rain Girl* (Nsemia Inc., 2019) followed in 2019.

Okemwa has participated in many poetry festivals around the world, including the 20th International Poetry Festival in Medellin (Colombia) in 2010. He was a guest poet at the 27th Biennale Poetry Festival in Liege (Belgium) in 2012; a guest-poet in the 3rd Spring and Poetry Festival in Istanbul (Turkey) in 2018; a visiting poet at the International Poetry Festival of Hanoi (Vietnam) in 2019; and was a creative writing resident at Faber Writers' Residency in Catalonia (Spain) in 2019. The residency in Catalonia gave birth to the collection of poems, *Love from Afro Catalonia*.

In 2018 Okemwa earned a doctorate in Literature from Moi University, Kenya, with a dissertation titled *A Study of the Kwani? Open Mic 'Literary-Gangsta' Performance Poetry of Kenya*. He also holds a Masters' degree in literature and a Bachelor of Education degree from the University of Nairobi, Kenya.

Foreword

It is a great honour to write a foreword for this pioneer work titled, *Oral Poetry in Africa: the Abagusii of Kenya* by Dr. Christopher Okemwa. This is one title, among the more than ten books, Okemwa has published in the field of Oral Literature and other related areas. The publication of these works clearly demonstrates the enthusiasm and commitment that Okemwa has in documenting the cultural heritage and history of the Abagusii people.

Poetry in the Abagusii community, as the case is in other African societies, was majorly sung. This is what is referred to as oral poetry since the songs were not written down, but were passed by word of mouth from one generation to the other. In this regard, due to the rapid changes in the world that are largely driven by external influences, there is real danger that such a rich and unique heritage could disappear without trace unless it is written. It is within this understanding that Dr. Okemwa has composed this seminal book on the oral literature of the Abagusii people.

However, the documentation of this oral poetry cannot be complete without the performance of the same. As Ruth H. Finnegan (1976) in her book, *Oral Literature in Africa,* observes "oral literature depends on a performer who formulates it in words on a specific occasion--- there is no other way in which it can be realized as a literary product." Thus, oral poetry in a written form is dead on the page, until such a time when a performer sings the poem. Consequently, it can be argued that in its written form, a reader of a poem, cannot have the physical expression and gestures that are made by a performer; the reactions and role of the audience; the accompanying musical instruments, and; the noise and sounds --- yet it is all these facets that contribute towards the production of meaning in oral poetry.

It should also be emphasized that since oral poetry of the Abagusii community, as the case is in most other African societies, is threatened by extinction, it is only in its written form that Literary Scholars, such as Okemwa can capture and preserve it for posterity. Indeed, this forms the basis upon which physical performance of the same can be developed and realized, now and in the future. I, therefore, applaud and commend this noble effort of presenting Gusii oral poetry in its written form by Dr. Okemwa.

Furthermore, it is important to note that oral poetry in the Abagusii community covered every facet of community life. The community's socio-political and economic life, history, values, norms and customs were stored in the oral poetry, as well as in the proverbs, riddles and folktales. In this regard, oral poetry was sung during different occasions including during child birth, initiation, marriage and burial ceremonies. As Finnegan (1976) observes:

> In the traditional African society, the poetry is specifically 'occasional', in that they are designed for, and arises from particular situations like funerals, weddings, celebrations of victory, soothing a baby, accompanying work, and so on (Finnegan, 1976:12).

In other words, oral poetry did not exist as art-for-art's sake, but as art for a particular purpose. Thus, in postulating the functions of poetry in the Abagusii community, Abai (2015) states that the Abagusii poems:

> ... were short emotional songs sang during special occasions (e.g., on wedding days, and circumcision ceremonies). Each poem had its particular message to convey (Abai, 2015:198).

Consequently, oral poetry in African societies such as the Abagusii was functional and tackled pertinent issues of a particular historical and cultural moment. It was through oral poetry that the community lived and survived.

Thus, in this book, Dr. Okemwa, has explored different aspects of Abagusii people's lives and the oral poetry that accompanied diverse aspects and events. For instance, Dr. Okemwa examines the poetry sung during child birth, and by extension explores the significance of child birth in the Abagusii community. Also, he analyzes the poetry sung during initiation ceremonies for both girls and boys. In addition, he examines the poetry associated with marriage ceremonies, including before, during and after courtship. He makes an elucidation of the poetry of war and skirmishes between the Gusii and belligerent neighbouring ethnic communities such as the Maasai, Kipsigis and Luo. Furthermore, historical events, including immigration and settlement of the Abagusii people are discussed at length. The *emeino* songs (Gusii classical lyrics) are presented.

Last, but not least, while this book is meant for students of oral literature at university level, it is also recommended for individuals or groups that research on African oral literature, African culture, anthropology, history and sociology. Indeed, the book is good for the general readership interested in the history and culture of the Abagusii.

Prof. John S. Akama, PhD.
Vice-Chancellor, Kisii University

Preface

Oral literature material among the Abagusii of Kenya is on the verge of extinction. According to UNESCO, *Ekegusii* (the language spoken by Abagusii) is one of the languages in the world that is on the verge of dying away and may disappear all the same. This is because most parents in Gusii (the land of Abagusii) encourage their children to learn 'prestigious' languages, like English and Kiswahili, while discouraging them from using their mother tongue. Some schools, too, punish students who speak in *Ekegusii*.

If this trend continues, as it is likely to do, *Ekegusii* language will die totally in the very near future. The looming extinction of the language would have a major negative impact upon the Abagusii as a people: facets of Omogusii culture will be lost from the face of the world; there will be no language to express Omogusii stories and history; and, in totality, the identity of Abagusii as a people will be lost and the world will be poorer culturally.

That is why I have, rather enthusiastically, researched into *Ekegusii* language, literature and history and have published the following books: *Riddles of the Abagusii of Kenya: Gems of Wisdom from the African Continent* (Nsemia Inc., 2011), *Proverbs of the Abagusii of Kenya: Meaning & Application* (Nsemia Inc., 2012), *Otenyo, the Hero of the Abagusii* (Nsemia Inc., 2016), *Ogasusu na Okanyang'au, Ogasusu na Oganchogu, Ogasusu na Okanyambu, Kerangeti na Kerantina*, and *Okang'ombe, Okanyang'au, Ogangware na Ogakondo* (Kistrech Theatre International, 2015). I belief these publications will help (even in a small way) to preserve the *Ekegusii* culture, language, literature and history.

Oral poetry exists in performance. It cannot be realized in written form until it is performed. However, I have captured it in this written form with the believe that it will be preserved for posterity. Further research is required on how to preserve its performances. One approach would be to have the poetry transcribed in musical notation so as to safeguard the poetry's original tunes from being changed or tampered with. I hope someone will do this as a matter of urgency.

Snippets of oral poetry of the Abagusii can be found in past researches, such as *The Making of Man and Woman under Abagusii Customary Laws* by Nelson King'oina Nyang'era (1999); 'Analysis of Symbolism and Transience in the Oral Literature of Abagusii of Western Kenya' by Felix Orina Oyioka (2014); *The History and Traditions of Abagusii of Kenya: Mwanyagetinge* by Abai Ochoi (2015); *The Gusii of Kenya: Social, Economic, Cultural, Political & Judicial Perspectives* by John S. Akama (Nsemia Inc. 2017) and *The Untold Story: Gusii Survival Techniques and Resistance to the Establishment of British Colonial Rule* by John S. Akama (2018). However, a comprehensive collection and analysis of the genre has not been done. This book is an attempt at bringing together the Abagusii oral poetry of birth, circumcision, marriage, old age, death, work, immigration, settlement, inter-clan and inter-ethnic skirmishes and wars.

Mine has been an attempt to collect as much as I could manage to collect of Abagusii oral poetry. In no way can I claim that this collection and analysis of this oral poetry is exhaustive. I am sure there is oral poetry out there that is not included in this book and which did not come to my attention. As well, I am sure there are other intepretations that differ from some of those I present here. As such, more research is needed to unearth unknown pieces of oral poetry within the community and the analysis. For instance, chants in this book seem to come from Bogirango and Nyaribari clans, and hardly any from Bonchari, Bobasi, Kitutu and Machoge. A similar study can endeavour to interrogate the chants, or their variations, from these clans.

General Oral Poetry

This book tackles the general oral poetry. As has been observed above by John Akama in his foreword, oral poetry was occasional and covered the community's social-political and economic life, history, values, norms and customs. These aspects of life were stored, not only in the oral poetry, but also in proverbs, riddles and folktales.

First, we see from this book that oral poetry was used to serve as a historical storage. It recorded, preserved and passed on the people's experiences. The Gusii oral poetry also communicated Abagusii's philosophy, as in the oral piece, *Mogisankio akoreke ekee*. As a socializer, the poetry provided guidelines on behaviour. It promoted good qualities, such as honesty, kindness, hard work, bravery, and generosity while condemning bad characteristics, such as selfishness, jealousy, envy, and others like these. We also note that the oral poetry was a store of cultural materials. Oral poetry, indeed, coloured the entire journey of a Gusii life – birth, circumcision, marriage and death.

One notable thing one learns from the oral poetry in this book is its improvisational nature. An artist performs a piece of poem as he composes it, or composes it as he performs it. The text of the poem is not fixed but ephemeral. The poet could add or subtract from the poem depending on whether the audience is in love with his performance and wants more or depending on the time available for the performance or on situations that arise at that time of performance.

Since the poetry rose from an occasion, it could pick events, happenings, or issues in the community and weave them into its text and performance. That is why we can conclude that the oral poetry of the Abagusii, and indeed that of other African communities, was not permanent, but ephemeral. It was new each time it was performed.

Miruka (1994) notes that the oral performance in many African communities is not a mere reproduction of rehearsed material. He refers to this expansive aspect as 'elasticity' or, as Ruth Finnegan (1976) puts it, 'verbal variability.' This aspect of 'elasticity' or 'verbal variability' is explained further by Finnegan: "What might be called the 'same' poem or prose piece tends to be variable to such an extent that one has to take some account at least of the original contribution of the artist actualizing it – and not simply in terms of technique of delivery" (Finnegan: 1976:8).

'Verbal variability' or 'elasticity' (Finnegan 1976; Miruka 1994) is an aspect that enables an artist to improvise on his/her performance and composition. This verbal variability leads to a new version of a piece of poetry being produced – different from the original.

We can, therefore, conclude that the oral poetry of the Abagusii is not fixed and is not permanent. A performer adds and subtracts from a poem. As the reader will note, the general oral poetry in this book is different from the *emeino* (clasiscal lyrics) that we shall discuss in this work. While the general oral poetry is ephemeral and improvisational, the *emeino* are fixed forms.

Emeino - *(Classical Lyrics of the Abagusii)*

Emeino (singular: *omoino*) were formulated poems which, unlike general oral poetry dicussed above, does not change. In other words, a performer cannot add or subtract from *omoino*. While other oral poems employed improvisations, in which the poet could add his/her own flavour to the lyrics, *emeino* were fixed classicals and were to be sung the way they were originally composed. *Emeino* were specially sung by old people, usually men, when drinking or engaging in partying. Young people and women did not compose or sing *emeino*.

It is said that an old man in the Gusii community was expected to have skill of composing and singing *emeino*. It was sad and unfortunate for an old man who had not acquired such a creative skill. As the following poem suggests, such a man was looked down upon and ridiculed.

Mogaka Otachi Meino	**An Elder who Can't Sing Emeino**
Mogaka otachi 'meino	An elder who can't sing *emeino*
Agende mwa Kwamboka o'Biranya	Should visit Kwamboka o'Biranya
Asibore emeino n'ebitonga	And fetch a basket full of poems
Achie kona gotera mwaye	He could sing the poems when back at home
Aaa eee	Aaa eee
Aaa eee	Aaa eee
Oyio n'omogaka otachi meino- eee	That is the old man who cannot sing, eee
Oyio n'omogaka otachi meino- eee	That is the old man who cannot sing, eee
Obe-aaa eee	Obe-aa ee

(Orina: 2014).

Abai (2015) has documented a similar classical poem in his book titled "Otachi Meino Aye Tocha Minto" and "Osangore Emeino n'Ebitonga" which also highlight the value attached to the composition and singing of *emeino* by the Abagusii. Let us examine the two compositions:

Otachi Meino Aye Tocha Minto	**Since You Can't sing Classical Songs, You are Not Welcome to Our Home**
Eee botambe ningokania	I always tell you
Otachi meino aye tocha minto	Since you can't sing *emeino* do not come to our home
Eee botambe ningokania	I do not welcome you
Otachi meino aye tocha minto	Since you can't sing *emeino* do not come to our home
Otachi meino aye tocha minto	Since you can't sing *emeino* do not come to our home
Ebisora nyameino bache minto	Only those who can sing come to our home
Bache minto	Come to our home
Bache minto	Come to our home
'Bisora nyameino bache minto	Only those who can sing come to our home
Bache minto	Come to our home
Bache minto	Come to our home
'Bisora nyameino bache minto	Only those who can sing come to our home
Oraiiya, oraiya	Oraiiya-a, oraiya-ta
Chingero bonyangero – taa!	Song of songs –taa!

(Abai:2015)

Osangore Emeino n'Ebitonga	**Collect a Full basket of Emeino**
Eee onye aye tochi meino	Eee, if you can't sing *emeino*
Ogende o'Kwamboka o Miranyi	Go to the home of Kwamboka o'Miranyi
Eee onye aye tochi meino	Eee, if you can't sing *emeino*
Ogende o Kwamboka o Miranyi	Go to the home of Kwamboka o'Miranyi
Ogende o Kwamboka o Miranyi	Go to the home of kwamboka o'Miranyi
Osangore emeino n'ebitonga	Collect a full basket of *emeino*

N'ebitonga	Full basket
N'ebitonga	Full basket
Osangore emeino n'ebitonga	Collect a full basket of *emeino*
N'ebitonga	Full basket
N'ebitonga	Full basket
Osangore emeino n'ebitonga	Collect a full basket of *emeino*
Oraiiya-a, oraiiya-a	Oraiiya-a, oraiya-a
Chingero bonyangero – taa	Song of songs – taa

(Orina: 2014)

According to Orina (2014) an old man in the Abagusii community was expected to compose and sing *emeino*. In the foregoing classical poems, a man who is handicapped in either singing or speaking the beautiful language of the people is 'advised to take lessons from a female member of the community who could sing better' (Orina: 2014). As Orina observes, nothing could be more unseemly than asking an elder to seek advice from a woman whatever the matter. What we gather from Orina, then, is that the acquisition of the skill to compose *emeino* and to be able to sing them was mandatory among the men in Gusii community. That tells us that *emeino* played a big role in the community and was part of people's life.

However, as much as the composition and the singing of *emeino* were important and mandatory among the Gusii men, it was not easy to acquire such a skill. Mzee Samwel Ombasa Tamaro explains that the composition and singing of *emeino* is called *okobinera emeino*. The word *okobinera* is derived from the word *okobina* which refers to the labour pain a woman experiences when giving or about to give birth. The composition and singing of *emeino* is equated to this pain since it requires a lot of effort in meditating and arranging words of the poem. Without pen, paper and computer, the old days saw a composer of such classical songs arrange words and stanzas in his head (memory), which was a difficult task compared to today's creative works in which artists jot down lines, or store them in the computer, for easy recollection. It is said that once a composer started composing *omoino*, he had to go all the way to the end of the composition. He did not compose in bits as artists do these days using computer, laptop, phone, pen and notebook.That is why it was not an easy task and that is why it was equated to *okobina* (a woman's labour pains).

The purpose of *emeino* was to praise those who had good virtues and had done acts of generosity, kindness and love. People whose deeds were extraordinarily good were sung in *emeino*. *Emeino* were also sung to condemn evil or bad deeds that vexed the community. Bad acts, misbehavior and habits were also disapproved through the singing of *emeino*. The *emeino* in this book, composed by our great grandfathers, were sung to me by Mzee Samuel Ombasa Tamaro who was formerly a teacher from Tabaka and Obino Nyambane who is the director of Culture in Kisii County.

There is another side of *emeino* fronted by Obino Nyambane (2018). According to him, *emeino* were social proverbs whose composition was as a result of a long period of experience. He states that this classical poetry of the Abagusii were sung in the evening for leisure after a long day of hard work. In this forum stories of the past, present and of the future were narrated. In this forum young men were told as follows:

Omomura omong'aini	An intelligent boy
Amigani amakere 'mogondo	Let him squeeze his ribs as he works hard on the farm
Amigani amakere 'mogondo	Squeeze his ribs as he works hard on the farm
Ching'ondi echio korwa Nyakongo	There comes sheep from Nyakongo

Obino explains that an intelligent man knew that hard work was a virtue that would put him at level with his age-group. He worked hard to have something to batter-trade with. *Ching'ondi echio korwa nyakongo* (there comes sheep from Nyakongo) here refers to sheep that are brought to the market to be exchanged in the batter trade. If a young man didn't work hard he will have nothing to exchange for the sheep.

Obino adds that *emeino* were also sung for self-praise, especially in the course of beer parties whereby the elders would coin words and make lyrics to summarize their lifestyles and experiences that could now serve as lessons and guidelines to younger generations.

Obino says that the old men used *emeino* to state who, among them, was better or more intelligent in the art of living. The contest or self-praise was done among *abagisangio/ekiare/ekegori* (age-mates). In the contest, whoever came out the best was to be emulated by the society or the young generation. The function of *emeino* in this case could be equated to the function of the present day *michongoano (sing. Mchongoano)* among young people in Schools.

The term *mchongoano is* derived from a Kiswahili verb "*chongoa*" which means, "to sharpen the edges of something" (Tuki, 2004). *Mchongoano* is defined as "a speech genre of playful verbal insults exchanged with an opponent and directed to another opponent directly or to his/her family members e.g. mother, sister, father, friends, girlfriend or boyfriend" (Kihara, 2013, p.101). It is "a Kenyan speech event very similar to what Americans call "playing the dozens." (Patrick C. Kihara and Helga Schröder, 2012, p.63-78). Ngugi (2010), on the other hand, defines '*mchongoano*' as "a type of sayings that are created or coined by pupils in primary and students in Secondary Schools" (Ngugi, 2010, p.8) whose function is to entertain the listeners, as well as to contest to see who coins a well-thought-out *mchongoano* than the others. Apart from socialization, *mchongoano's* main concern is humour (Githinji, 2007, pp.96-97; Kihara & Schröder (ibid.); it is a form of socialization with entertainment, education/information and observation skills embedded in it (Kihara, 2013, p.103). Just like *Mchongoano* whose function is to contest, *emeino* also is a contest of wits. Like *mchongoano,* the *emeino* also act as a socialization tool.

These beer-parties, where *emeino* were composed and sung, were attended by old men and sometimes by their sons who were younger. The events turned out to be recreational evenings characterized by chest-thumping, self-glorification, and contestation of out-doing one another –just as what happens in *mchongoano* sessions in Schools. During *emeino,* one elder would break into the following chant:

Obong'aini bw'egesibi	The intelligence of the sunbird
Tibonga bwa 'nyoni ende	Cannot be marched with that of any other bird
Obong'aini bw'egesibi	The intelligence of the sunbird
Tibonga bwa 'nyoni ende	Cannot be marched with that of any other bird
Tibonga bong'aini bwa 'nyoni ende	Cannot be marched with the intelligence of any other bird
Egesibi kenywa emete emekendu	The Sunbird that drinks water in the point where tree-branches intersect.

In this song the first elder, taking the image of *egesibi*, praises himself, saying that he is like *egesibi*. Using its beak, *egesibi* is known to drink water from the point where branches of a tree meet the main stem. It is believed that the water in this point is cold and medicinal, having washed down the leaves and boughs.

A second elder would come up to counter the first singer by singing the song *Egetinginye Ekeng'aini* (the clever wren) in an attempt to out-do the first old man. He will sing thus:

Egetinginye Ekeng'aini	**The Clever Wren**
Egetinginye ekeng'aini	The clever wren
Kerigia oboundi kiagache	Gathers twigs and grass, to built its nest
Embura egotwa gesoe mwaye	To shelter in when it rains
Egetinginye ekeng'aini	The clever wren
Kerigia oboundi kiagache	Gathers twigs and grass, to built its nest
Embura egotwa gesoe mwaye	To shelter in when it rains
Eee gesoe mwaye, ee baba	To shelter in, eh
Embura egotwa gesoe mwaye	To shelter in when it rains

Ee baba	Ee, baba
Embura egotwa gesoe mwaye	To shelter in when it rains
Embura egotwa gesoe mwaye	To shelter in when it rains

The oral poem states that the wren is a clever bird that builds its shelter before the rainy season starts. This elder equates himself with the bird to indicate that he is more intelligent than the first singer since, with him, he knows the seasons. He does things at their right times. He doesn't wait till it is too late. He constructs himself a house before the rainy season so that his family can shelter in it.

This contest among the old people was one of intelligence, experience and wisdom. The activity sometimes turned emotional and physical. According to Obino Nyambane the activity must have been the source of *endamwamu* (jealous). The good thing is that the contest had referees who controlled it and prevented such emotions from getting out of control. The referees took the responsibility of bringing things to an end when these emotions rose.

Obino Nyambane comments further that *emeino* contest opened ways for the elders to counsel, motivate, promote and put the society at an understanding level of equality for its own well-being. Whether a member of Abagusii community was like *egesibi* (Sun bird) who drunk 'cold water' (medicinal water) or was like *egetinginye ekeng'aini* (the clever wren), it did not matter since all these qualities were needed by the community for the well-being of its people.

We can, therefore, conclude that the composition and singing of *emeino* was an art that required innate talent and skill. Equated to birth-pain, the composition of *emeino* among men, served a big purpose of relaying experiences and wisdom to others. It promoted good virtues while it castigated bad characteristics.Despite its *mchongoano* nature, it did not matter who won in the contest of wits since, as has been noted, all the qualities carried in the oral poems were needed by the community for the well-being of its people.

Christopher Okemwa,
Author

Chapter 1
Poetry & Birth

The Role of Children in the Abagusii Society

Before we examine poetry sung during the birth of a child, let us look at the role of children in the Abagusii community. Children were at the centre of life in the Gusii community. Abagusii, like many communities across the world, placed a high value on children. Children were (and remain) the means via which a community perpetuated itself into the future. From a close scrutiny of Abagusii proverbs (see for example in the *Proverbs of the Abagusii of Kenya: Meaning & Application* (Okemwa: 2012)) it can be inferred that children were valued for many reasons, including the following:

(a) *Self-perpetuation*: Abagusii, like other African communities, begot children for purposes of self-perpetuation. Thus, we lived into perpetuity: our children begot children who also begot other children all the way into the future.

(b) *To defend the community:* As Abagusii say "*ensinyo manakobengwa 'mbamura etabwati*" meaning "when a community retreats and moves away from the border (usually due to harassment by the neighbouring community) it is an indication that the community lacks brave men to defend it." This means then that the Abagusii had to have children who would grow up to defend the community from external enemies.

Parents anticipated that their children (especially boys) would grow up to become *amarubi* (King cobras), who were fierce and could attack whoever dared to challenge the community into war. The proverb *omomura kare sobo ne'rirubi nyamong'ento* (a young man in a homestead is like a king cobra) (Okemwa:2012) summarises the importance of giving birth to (especially) boys in the community at that time.

(c) *To earn dowry:* Families in the Gusii community aspired to get girls to enable them get dowry when the girls were married off. A home with many daughters was perceived to be rich as it looked forward to fetch plenty of brideprice when they got married. This is captured in the proverb *monto ona mosubati omwabo, agende gesere kia'Nyamwamu, akunyorie mogoye ona kuoma, akore kerichi na kwabeka* (Okemwa:2012). In other words "let one with a sister go to Nyamwamu's forest-land and make a rope out of a tree bark and be ready to tie it round an animal". Families that had daughters were expected to ready themselves for windfall of wealth when the girls were married off. Another proverb, *enyomba y'abaiseke abange n'ekerandi getakwoma* (2012: Okemwa) meaning "a home with many girls is a gourd that never 'dries'". In the Gusii context, a dry gourd connotes destitution; a wet one (literary full of milk) implies the presence of plenty of food. In other words, a home with many girls (daughters) would, through the acquisition of dowry, always receive animals that will turn it into a wealthy, well-fed family.

(d) *To help with work in the family:* Families aspired to get many children so that they can help with various chores required to sustain the family. Mainstay tasks, such as farm work and animal rearing, were largely manual and hence required many hands. This is captured in the proverb *abange n'abaya nonya bariete kiane inkaigwa bororo* (many are good regardless of them being costly). In other words, even if many people (hands) consume a lot in terms of food or demand big payment for their labour, they are preferable as they accomplish more work.

(e) *Self-satisfaction:* Children brought self-satisfaction to their parents. There was no happiness in households without children. Adult men and women needed young ones so as to be fulfilled as parents. Abagusii say that *chimori ko chigotiria amakongo atengere* (when calves romp about with joy, the older cows watch with satisfaction). Nothing brought life's satisfaction to parents as much as children did.

(f) *To be respected:* Many people gave birth to children as a way of earning respect in the community. Those who did not have offspring were looked down upon while those who delayed to marry were seen as not very useful to the society. In the proverb *okoibora okuya gwakora 'mokungu 'monyaka enting'ana* (an immoral/dirty woman becomes a queen courtesy of her grown-up sons) tells us that children salvaged the reputation of otherwise despised members of the community, turning them into respectable people.

(g) *For identity purposes:* People love to see their own images through their children. Abagusii took pride in their children as captured in the humorous proverb *Eeri nyamagwari 'yang'o? Torochi eng'ina nyabisembe* (to whom does this spotted bull belong? Don't you see his checkered mother?) (Okemwa: 2012). One who did not have children did not have one's image and, therefore, was looked down upon.

(h) *To run errands:* Children helped parents run errands. In the old days, in the absence of modern transport, children walked long distances to deliver messages and fetch items needed by their parents or elders. Those who did not have children suffered a great deal. That is why Abagusii say that *Okoibora okobe nkwa nyoni etagotoma* (Okemwa: 2012) (A bird is not blessed if it has young ones who are unwilling to run errands for him/her).

From the preceding discussion it can be inferred that children were central to the existence and survival of the Abagusii community. A woman who got married was expected to give birth to (many) children. That is why an expectant woman was given unparalled care during pregnancy. She was exempted from heavy work like digging, carrying heavy loads or walking long distances. Everyone looked forward to see her have a baby.

Poetry during Birth
Mosamba Mwaye

When the baby came he/she was referred to as *mosamba mwaye*, meaning, one who has "burnt" or "destroyed" her/his hut/abode (womb). This *mosamba mwaye* is praised and loved for having successfully "burnt" her/his hut to come to the world. For that matter songs were sung in praise of him/her. Friends, relatives and neighbours visited the parents of the new-born baby to shower them with praises. As they held the new-born, they tossed him/her up and down while singing the song, *Mosamba Mwaye*.

Mosamba Mwaye	**One who has Burnt His/Her Hut**
Minamina Omboka	Work the hips as you praise
Motagotumia	One who has burnt his/her hut
Motagotumia mosamba mwaye---ee	Lift him/her, toss him/her up
Motagotumia	One who has burnt his/her hut, ee
Motagotumia mosamba mwaye---ee	One who has burnt his/her hut, ee
Mosamba mwaye	One who has burnt his/her hut
Komosamba mwaye	One who has burnt his/her hut
Tarera—ee	should not cry, ee
Mosamba mwaye	One who has burnt his/her hut
Komosamba mwaye	One who has burnt his/her hut
Tarera--ee	should not cry, ee

Chapter 2
Poetry for Children

Children in the Abagusii community, like those in other African societies, presented their oral poetry as play-songs or singing games. They made movements, danced, sung and made patterns using their hands, bodies and legs. Children's play-songs largely socialized the children through play and singing games. In addition to socialization, the children derived pleasure and entertainment from the play-songs.

Abagusii children play-songs utilized words and expressions that did not necessarily have meaning. According to Felix Orina Oyioka, words such as 'oombe' (oombe is the corrupted form of English 'Oh bae, oh baby', sung to lull the Whiteman's child to sleep) in *Omwana Arare* and *kambusi karangera* in the playsong "Kambusi Karangera" do not have any particular meaning. They were either borrowed by children from neighbouring communites, or were coined to create the desired rhythm or play patterns. Other words were just coined to help with tongue-twisting and enhance speech and skills in expressing oneself.

Most of the play-songs involved several children at a time who played the songs and created patterns. A few of the songs required one child to sing them and did not require the accompaniment or presence of other children. For example the Abagusii lullaby, "Omwana Arare" was sung by one person (probably a babysitter) to a child who was crying so as to sooth him/her to sleep.

Omwana Arare

The lullaby was sung to small children to soothe them to sleep. The poet (who could be a babysitter) gently patted the baby on its back as she sang the lullaby. The poet praised the child by telling it that it is a well-behaved baby. She told it that its mother would soon come, and when she came she would bring a banana for her/him. The repetition in the words "kira, kira kira" and "oombe, oombe" creates a musical rhythm that is calming and slowly soothes the small angel to sleep.

Omwana Arare	**Let the Baby Sleep**
Oombe, oombe	Oombe, oombe
Omwana arare	Let the baby sleep
Arare buya	Sleep peacefully
Chitoro chikomoreria	Sleep makes baby to whimper
Oombe, oombe	Oombe, oombe
Mama ngochare	Mummy is soon coming
Akorentere ritoke	Will bring you a banana
Oombe, oombe	Oombe, oombe
Omwana arare	Let the baby sleep
Arare buya	Sleep peacefully
Chitoro chikomoreria.	Sleep makes baby to whimper
Kira kira kira	Calm, calm, calm
Aye n'omuya	You are good
Ore omwana omuya	You are a good baby
Oombe, oombe	Oombe, oombe
Omwana arare	Let baby sleep
Arare buya	Sleep peacefully
Chitoro chikomoreria	Sleep makes baby to whimper

Baba Ominto n'Omuya

This oral poem, "Baba Ominto n'Omuya," was also sung by one child. In the song she/he praises the good care her/his mother gives her. The song was collected and translated by Felix Orina Oyioka (2014). The song goes as follows:

Baba Ominto n'Omuya	**My Mother is Good**
Baba ominto n'omuya	My Mother is good
Na tata ominto n'omuya	My father is also good
Baba ominto ondereire kwaa	My mother who raised me in her arms
Na magega aboronge	And on her back

Na ngobo chimarera	And in warm clothing
Baba okomanya kinomire	Mother who knows when I am starving
Namatori akoboko	Morsels ever ready at hand
Na 'tesibia	Even when she serves with dirty hands
Kogicha indie 'nyigote	I eat and fill my tummy
Baba nyambeere ibere	Mother, one with two breasts
Baba ominto amagenda tugutugu	Mother who crouches
Amagenda seremani	Walk sideways
Amagenda magunkuba	Crawls
Ko'chinda chioreka nsabo	All for my comfort

(Orina: 2014:191)

Kambusi Karanga

Typically children started socializing around the age of four. In their socialization they set riddles, told stories and also sung songs. The common song for children in the Abagusii community was *Kambusi Karanga*. The words in the song, as discussed previously, has no particular meaning, but must have been coined by children to just create rhythtm in their play-songs and help create patterns with their hands.

Kambusi Karanga	**Children's Singing Game**
Kambusi karanga	Roast the little cat
Nainche n'omorembo karanga	I am also beautiful, roast me
Nkagenda seito	I went to our home
Nkanyora akang'ina	I met an old woman
Gakang'a ebirwa	She gave me local brew
Nkaigwa n'ebiya	It was sweet
Ngaaka omonwa	I smarked my mouth
Ncha! Ncha!	Ncha! Ncha!
Meri ominto	My sister Mary
Masentero akare	Is living at Masentero
Koburugera ebiasi	Cultivating potatoes in a farm
Amo n'amaemba	And millet
Moraa endondo	Moraa endondo
Buna endondo endwe.	Like endondo endwe

This is a singing game, one of many, for children. They sung it in groups of four or thereabout, with their hands intertwined. They made different hand formations and patterns as they sang.

Nkagenda Mwabo Moraa

This is another Abagusii singing game played by children. The singer in the poem went to her/his friend's home and was given *ugali* that was not well-cooked with vegetables that had gone stale and this resulted in an upset stomach, leading to diarrhear (indicated by the ideophone *sia, sia siaraa!*). The poem, employing satire, is meant to create humour and make the children at play laugh at the singer. It is meant to generate laughter and make fun of those who eat without constraint.

The poem has a rhyming nature, thus the lines end with words, such as 'bototo' and 'ngundo,' whose last syllables have similar sounds. This rhyming nature of words creates rhythm suitable for dancing and singing by the children.

Nkagenda Mwabo Moraa	**I Visited Moraa**
'Nkagenda mwabo Moraa	I went to Moraa's home
'Nkaria 'bokima 'bototo	I ate ugali not fully cooked
N'amabere 'mayio	With unfermented milk
Na'nderema 'ngundo	And stale vegetables
Sia, sia, siaraaaaaa!	Sia, sia, siaraaaaaa!
'Nkagenda mwabo Moraa	I went to Moraa's home
'Nkaria 'bokima 'bototo	I ate ugali not fully cooked
N'amabere 'mayio	With unfermented milk
Na'nderema 'ngundo	And stale vegetables
Sia, sia, siaraaaaaa!	Sia, sia, siaraaaaaa!

Ekero Narenge Omwana

This oral poem, "Ekero Narenge Omwana" is a popular song in Gusii. It recollects memories of childhood.

Ekero Narenge Omwana	**When I was Young**
Ekero narenge omwana	I was prohibited
Obe inkanigwa, baba	I was prohibited

Christopher Okemwa

Ekero narenge omwana	When I was young
Obee inkanigwa, ee	I was prohibited
Ekero narenge omwana	When I was young
Obe inkanigwa, baba	I was prohibited
Ekero narenge omwana	When I was young
Obee inkanigwa, ee	I was prohibited
Inkanigwa timbaisa koria	Prohibited from eating
Amara, baba	Intestines, oh!
Inkanigwa timbaisa koria	Prohibited from eating
Amara, baba, ee	Intestines, baba, ee!
Inkanigwa timbaisa koria	Prohibited from eating
Amara, baba	Intestines, oh!
Inkanigwa timbaisa koria	Prohibited from eating
Amara, baba, ee	Intestines, baba, ee!
Nkoria amara, obe nintamue	If I eat, I will become disobedient
Baba	Baba
Inkoria amara, obe nintamue	If I eat, I will become disobedient
Ee, ee	Eee
Nkoria amara, obe nintamue	If I eat, I will become disobedient
Baba	Baba
Inkoria amara, obe nintamue	If I eat, I will become disobedient
Ee, ee	Eee
Nkachia gotiga, baba	So, I stopped eating, eh!
Nkachia gotiga e-e	So, I stopped eating, eh!
Koria amara, baba	Intestines, eh!
Nkachia gotiga e-e	So, I stopped eating, ee
Ng'a nintamue, baba	That I will become disobedient
Ngachia gotiga e-e	So, I stopped eating, ee
Ekero narenge omwana	When I was young
Tata agantebia	My father told me

Yara gachie orisie	Son, go and graze (animals)
Ndisia rituko boira	I grazed them for the whole day
Ekero banyenya	But when they slaughtered
Ankania 'ng'a tindi amara	They will refuse me eating intestines
Ntangori ndero	I wish it were today!
Baba konainyoire	Eh, when I remember
Ntangori ndero	I wish it were today
Baba ee rituko boira	Eh, the whole day
Tangori ndero	I wish it were today
Eee ntangori ndero, ee, ee	Ee, ee, I wish it were today
Ntangori ndero	Ee, ee, I wish it were today
Ekero narenge omwana	When I was young
Obe inkanigwa, baba	I was prohibited, oh!
Ekero narenge omwana	When I was young
Obee inkanigwa, ee	Oh! I was prohibited
Ekero narenge omwana	When I was young
Obe inkanigwa, baba	I was prohibited, oh!
Ekero narenge omwana	When I was young
Obee inkanigwa, ee	Oh! I was prohibited
Inkanigwa, timbaisa koria	I was prohibited from eating
Amani, baba	Liver, eh!
Inkanigwa timbaisa koria	I was prohibited from eating
Amani, baba, ee	Liver, eh!
Inkanigwa timbaisa koria	I was prohibited from eating
Amani, baba	Liver, eh!
Inkanigwa timbaisa koria	I was prohibited from eating
Amani, baba, ee	Liver, baba, eh!
Nkoria amani	If I eat liver
Obe nintamue, baba	I will become disobedient, oh!
Nkoria amani	If I eat liver
Obe nintamue, ee	I will become disobedient, oh!

Nkoria amani	If I eat liver
Obe nintamue, baba	I will become disobedient, oh!
Nkoria amani	If I eat liver
Obe nintamue, ee	I will become disobedient, oh!
Nkachia gotiga, baba	So, I stopped, oh!
Nkachia gotiga, ee	I stopped eating, ee
Koria amani, baba	Eating liver, oh!
Nkachia gotiga, ee	I stopped eating e-e
Ng'a nintamue, baba	That eating will make me disobedient
Nkachia gotiga, ee	I stopped eating, eh!
Ekero narenge omwana	When I was young
Tata agantebia	Father told me
Yara gachie orisie	Son, go graze (animals)
Ndisia rituko boira	I grazed the whole day
Ekero banyenya	But when they slaughtered
Angania ng'a tindi amani	He refused me eating liver
Ntangori ndero	I wish it were today
Baba, ee, konainyoire	Baba, eh, when I remember
Ntangori ndero	I wish it were today
Baba, ee, rituko boira	Baba, eh, whole day
Ntangori ndero	I wish it were today
Ee, ee ntangori ndero	Ee, ee, I wish it were today
Ee, ee, ntangori ndero	Ee, ee, I wish it were today

This song sung by adults brings memories of childhood. It is a demonstration of how young boys' obedience and patience were tested. A boy could tend cattle for days on end, but when one of the cows was slaughtered he was prohibited from eating the sweetest/best parts of the kill--the entrails. We speculate that the prohibition was to tempt him into disobedience. The objective of this 'temptation' was intended to reinforce obedience in children. If a boy was really obedient he would still do his duty of looking after the cows even when he was banned from eating the delicious entrails. The song captures the message of boys' obedience and hard work without questioning authority while demonstrating perseverance and endurance. They were encouraged to work without expecting a reward in return. It was believed that any pampering of the boys could lead to disobedience and laziness. Staying tough on them would ensure they remained obedient and continue working hard, even when they received nothing in return.

Obino Nyambane, who is a specialist in the Oral poetry of the Abagusii, adds that if the boys were allowed to eat the delicious parts of the slaughtered animal it could lead to destruction in the field. This is because if they were allowed to eat the prohibited parts, eg liver, intestines, gizzard, etc, it could lead them to discover the sweetness in them. This sweetness could tempt the boys to secretly kill the animals and remove the entrails (the sweetest parts) and eat them. Therefore, to avoid it all together, the elders instilled the law that prohibited them from eating the entrails.

Irongo mwa Nyamboye

This *omoino* (classical poem) was sung to me by Samwel Ombasa Tamaro (2017). It talks about a man called Kemanwa who, when hungry, climbed up the loft of the house of Nyamboye to steal meat kept for a child. He was with his friend Keure. When he was caught he said that he was looking for oil which he was to apply on his skin.

Irongo mwa Nyamboye	Up the Loft at Nyamboye's Hut
Irongo	Up the loft
Mwanyamboye, Kemanwa ee baba	At Nyamboye's kemanwa, ee
Irongo	Up the loft
Mwanyamboye, Kemanwa ee baba	At Nyamboye's kemanwa, ee
Irongo	Up the loft
Mwanyamboye, ninki okorigia irongo	At Nyamboye's, what are you looking for?
Irongo	Up the loft
Mwanyamboye, ninki okorigia irongo	At Nyamboye's, what are you looking for?
Irongo	Up the loft
Mwanyamboye	At Nyamboye's
Kemanwa orire enyama--ureeee!	Kemanwa has eaten meat—ureeee
Kemanwa orire enyama--ureeee!	Kemanwa has eaten meat—ureeee

Orire enyama y'omwana	Has eaten a child's meat
Irongo	Up the loft
Mwanyamboye, Kemanwa ee baba	At Nyamboye's kemanwa, ee
Irongo	Up the loft
Mwanyamboye orire enyama y'omwana	At Nyamboye's, he has eaten a child's meat
Irongo	Up the loft
Mwanyamboye orire enyama y'omwana	He has eaten a child's meat
Irongo	Up the loft
Mwanyamboye, ning'o omosangameire?	At Nyamboye's, who was with him?
Irongo	
Mwanyamboye, ning'o omosangameire?	At Nyamboye's, who was with him?
Irongo	Up the loft
Mwanyamboye, ning'o omosangameire?	At Nyamboye's, who was with him?
Irongo	
Mwanyamboye, Keureee baba	At Nyamboye's, he was with Keure
Irongo	Up the loft
Mwanyamboye, Keureee baba	At Nyamboye's, he was with Keure
Irongo	

Irongo mwanyamboye	Up the loft at Nyamboye's
Irongo mwa nyamboye	Up the loft at Nyamboye's
Irongo mwanyamboye	Up the loft at Nyamboye's
Irongo mwa nyamboye	Up the loft at Nyamboye's

Kemanwa orire enyama--ureeee!	Kemanwa has eaten meat—ureeee
Kemanwa orire enyama--ureeee!	Kemanwa has eaten meat—ureeee
Orire enyama y'omwana	Has eaten a child's meat
Irongo	Up the loft

Mwanyamboye, Keureee baba	At Nyamboye's, Keureee
Irongo	Up the loft
Mwanyamboye, ning'o omosangameire?	At Nyamboye's, who was with him?
Irongo	Up the loft

Irongo mwanyamboye	Up the loft at Nyamboye's
Irongo mwa nyamboye	Up the loft at Nyamboye's
Irongo mwanyamboye	Up the loft at Nyamboye's
Irongo mwa nyamboye	Up the loft at Nyamboye's
Girango techi kende	
Irongo	Up the loft
Girango techi kende	
Irongo	Up the loft
N'omoiri bache goita	
Irongo	Up the loft
N'omoiri bache goita	
Irongo	Up the loft
Irongo mwa nyamboye	Up the loft at Nyamboye's
Irongo mwa nyamboye	Up the loft at Nyamboye's
Irongo mwa nyamboye	Up the loft at Nyamboye's
Kemanwa orire enyama--ureeee!	Kemanwa has eaten meat--ureeee
Kemanwa orire enyama--ureeee!	Kemanwa has eaten meat--ureeee
Orire enyama y'omwana	Has eaten a child's meat
Irongo	Up the loft
Mwanyamboye orire enyama y'omwana	At Nyamboye's, he has eaten a child's meat
Irongo	Up the loft
Mwanyamboye, ning'o omosangameire?	At Nyamboye's, he has eaten a child's meat
Irongo	Up the loft
Nkeure ee baba nere omosang'ameire	It was Keure, ee, who was with him
Irongo mwa nyamboye x2	Up the loft at Nyamboye's
Irongo mwanyamboye	Up the loft at Nyamboye's
Irongo mwanyamboye	Up the loft at Nyamboye's
Irongo mwanyamboye	Up the loft at Nyamboye's

Christopher Okemwa

Ntakoreti Kinde Omoke

This song, "Ntakoreti Kinde Moke" (Orina: 2014: 186) was collected and translated by Felix Orina Oyioka. The poet in the song is an adult who recalls the strength and ability he had when he was a young person.

Ntakoreti Kinde Omoke	**When I was Young**
Inguru chiamang'aine chiaguto	With ant bear's yoked strength
A 'ng'era	Like a rhino
Ko nechia'nchogu eguatia 'mbara	Or an elephant splitting planks
Monto ankori moke	If I were to be young again
Monyenche bw'amaguta	Easy and flexible like cooking oil and
Moseto ko morere	With my marrow young and tender
Nare kominyoka 'nkobongia	I'd run and pick things simultaneously
Nkorama kande anchera ntiga	I could insult and injure
Anchera gateneine buna gete kiandara	Leaving the feeble erect like lone sticks
Akagokwa gakwa	The weak ones dying
Na'agakoba kaba	And the strong surviving

(Orina: 2014)

Ntare Koba Omomura

This oral poem, "'Ntare Koba Momura," was sung by a girl. The girl singing the song wished that she was born a boy! If she were a boy she could drive her father's cow to the river. Note that in Gusii only boys could tend to cows and other livestock. This girl in the song must have admired what the boys did when they drove the cows to the river: whistling to the cow, telling her to drink water, and then driving her home after drinking the water. Cows were paid as dowry, the boys are the ones to pay the dowry. This behoved them to tend the cattle well. The girl's lament is based on the thought that one day she will never leave her parents' home. She wishes she were a boy to live at her home 'forever').

Ntare Koba Omomura	**I Wish I were a Boy**
Ntare koba omomura	I wish I were a boy
Ng'ire nyang'era roche	So I drive our cow to the river
Ng'ire nyang'era roche	I drive our cow to the river

15

Inyebugerie egechuria	I whistle for her
Inyebugerie egechuria	I whistle for her
Nyang'era kanywe amache	Nyang'era, drink water
Nyang'era kanywe amache	Drink water
Totire egetiro	Then we walk up the hill
Iye yeiye, 'ntare koba omomura	*Iye yeiye*, I wish I were a boy
Iye yeiye, 'ntare koba omomura	*Iye yeiye*, I wish I were a boy.

Genda Roche Nyamoita One

This oral poem was sung by a mother to her daughter. She tells her in the song to be careful as she goes to the river to fetch water. In the water are frogs that are stubborn and on the way home are creepers or undergrowth that are stubborn as well. In other words, there are lots of challenges she had to expect. Some people argue that this poem is alluding to premarital sex that the girls risked being involved in while away from the vicinity of their parents. In those days boys waylaid young girls on their way to the river. They will either rape them or persuade them to do sex with them in the bushes. Therefore, the oral poem is a warning from the mother to the girl to steer clear of such acts.

Genda Roche Nyamoita One	**Go to the River My Daughter Nyamoita**
Genda roche Nyamoita one	Nyamoita my daughter go to the river
Gachie roche	Go to the river
Genda roche Nyamoita one	Nyamoita my daughter go to the river
Gachie roche	Go to the river
Obuche Amaya, amakenonoku	Fetch good and clean water
Obuche Amaya, amakenonoku	Fetch good and clean water
Genda roche Nyamoita one	Nyamoita my daughter go to the river
Gachie roche	Go to the river
Obuche ng'ora	Fetch carefully
Nyamoita one obuche ng'ora	Nyamoita my daughter fetch carefully
Obuche ng'ora	Fetch carefully
Nyamoita one obuche ng'ora	Nyamoita my daughter fetch carefully

Otire ng'ora	Come back carefully
Nyamoita one otire ng'ora	Nyamoita my daughter come back carefully
Otire ng'ora	Come back carefully
Nyamoita one otire ng'ora.	Nyamoita my daughter come back carefully
Emerande 'nchera n'emekorekanu	Creepers on the path are intertwined
Emerande nchera n'emekorekanu	Creepers on the path are intertwined
Otire ng'ora	Come back carefully
Nyamoita one otire ng'ora.	Nyamoita my daughter come back carefully
Kogoika nyomba Nyaboke tasaba mache	When you get home
	Nyaboke should not ask for water
Kogoika nyomba Nyaboke tasaba mache	When you get home
	Nyaboke should not ask for water
Nomotamu mono, n'omoburaburu	She is so disobedient, so obstinate
Nomotamu mono, n'omoburaburu	When you get home
Kogoika nyomba Nyaboke tasaba mache.	Nyaboke should not ask for water

Chiana Kerario Boira

Last-born boys in the Abagusii community were known to be pampered, tolerated and over-protected by their parents. Because of this they became rude, proud and sometimes irresponsible. The following *omoino* (classical poem) is about a last-born boy in one of the families in Gusii. The elder brothers complained about him being stubborn, but the mother came to his protection and asked them to leave him alone. When the father came home one day, he found that the cows that this last-born boy was supposed to tend, were left on their own in the fields and had not been fed or taken to the river to drink water. That is when this old man sung this chant. The word *kerario* refers to the spot in the field on which the cows are teethered.

Ee chiana 'kerario boira	**They Moo the Whole Day**
Ee chiana 'kerario boira	They moo in the fields the whole day
Chiombe chiana 'kerario boira	Cows moo in the fields the whole day
Ee chiana 'kerario boira	Ee moo in the fields the whole day
E chiombe chiana 'kerario boira	E cows moo in the fields the whole day

Chiombe chiana 'kerario boira	Cows moo in the fields the whole day
'Ng'ai omokogoti agachiete?	Where has the last-born gone?
Ee chiana 'kerario boira	Ee they moo in the fields the whole day
Chiombe chiana 'kerario boira	Cows moo in the fields the whole day
Chiana 'kerario boira	They moo in the fields the whole day
Chiombe chiana 'kerario boira	Cows moo in the fields the whole day
E chiombe chiana 'kerario boira	E cows moo in the fields the whole day
'Ng'ai omokogoti agachiete?	Where has the last-born gone?
E agachiete, ere agachiete	E where has he gone, has he gone?
'Ng'ai omokogoti agachiete?	Where has the last-born gone?
E agachiete	E gone
'Ng'ai omokogoti agachiete?	Where has the last-born gone?
E agachiete	E gone
'Ng'ai omokogoti agachiete?	Where has the last-born gone?
Chiana kerario boira	They moo in the fields the whole day
Chiombe chiana kerario boira	Cows moo in the fields the whole day
Chiana kerario boira	They moo in the fields the whole day
Chiombe chiana kerario boira	Cows moo in the fields the whole day
Chiombe chiana boira	Cows moo in the fieds the whole day
'Ng'ai omokogoti agachiete?	Where has he gone?
Oraiyaa, oraiyaa	Oraiyaa, oraiyaa
Etago yane omosaiga.	Etago, my friend

Omwana Ona Ng'ina na Ise

This *omoino* was sung by orphans and widows. They envied the lives of children with both parents. The two say that such children are fed the whole day because food is plenty in their homes.

Omwana Ona Ng'ina na Ise	**A Child with a Mother and a Father**
Ee omwana ona ng'ina na ise	Ee, a child with a mother and a father
Omwana ona ng'ina na iseee	Child with mother and a father---eeee
Ee omwana ona ng'ina na ise	Ee with a mother and a father
Omwana ona ng'ina na ise	A child with a mother and a father
Aragerigwe bokaira--aaaa	Is fed the whole day---aaaa
Ee omwana ona ng'ina na ise	Ee, a child with a mother and a father
Omwana ona ng'ina na ise-eee	Child with a mother and a father--eeee
Ee omwana ona ng'ina na ise	Ee, a child with a mother and a father
Omwana ona ng'ina na ise	A child with a mother and a father
Aragerigwe bokaira--aaaa	Is fed the whole day--aaaa
Ee omwana ona ng'ina na ise--aaaa	Ee, a child with a mother and a father--aaaa
Aragerigwe bokaira--aaaa	He/she is fed the whole day--aaaaa
Ee k'ebinto bi'mosungo--aaaa	Food dangles from the roof--a plenty--aaaa
Ee k'ebinto bi'mosungo--aaaa	Food dangles from the roof--a plenty--aaaa

Ekiora 'Mbago Mogaka

Mzee Samwel Ombasa Tamaro tells me a tale (2017): A long time ago in a place called Mesesi, Bogirango Clan, in Gusii, there was a boy who was so violent that he broke enclosures to steal his father's cows. He forced his father, Masenge, to give him more cows in addition to those he had forcibly taken. People were not happy. His father, his brothers and the community people beat him thoroughly. He ran away to live in Bokione and Boochi in Bomachoge. His descendants live there to date. His clansmen composed the following *omoino* that was about him.

Ekiora 'mbago omogaka	**A Fence-Breaker**
Ekiora 'mbago omogaka	A renegade fence-breaker
Mbabuna obonda na Masenge	Forced wealth from his father

Ekiora 'mbago omogaka	A renegade fence-breaker
Mbabuna obonda na Masenge	Forced wealth from his father
Mbabuna obonda na Masenge	Forced wealth from his father
Obonda Masenge bwarabeire	The wealth that Masenge has now recovered
Ee bwarabeire, e bwarabeire	Ee he has recovered, has recovered
Obonda Masenge bwarabeire	The wealth Masenge has recovered
Bwarabeire	Has recovered
Obonda Masenge bwarabeire	The wealth Masenge has received
Bwarabeire	Has recovered
Obonda Masenge bwarabeire-eee	The wealth Masenge has recoved
Ekiora 'mbago omogaka	A renegade fence-breaker
Mbabuna obonda na Masenge	Forced wealth from his father
Ekiora 'mbago omogaka	A renegade fence-breaker
Mbabuna obonda na Masenge	Forced wealth from his father
Mbabuna obonda na Masenge	Forced wealth from his father
Obonda Masenge bwarabeire-eeee	The wealth that Masenge has now recovered
Oraiyaa, oraiyaa	Oraiyaa, oraiyaa
Chingero bonyangero-ta!	Songs of songs-ta!

Chapter 3
Poetry for Circumcision Ceremonies

Circumcision for both boys and girls was practised by the Abagusii as a rite of passage. An uncircumcised boy was scornfully (perjoratively) referred to as *omoisia*. A girl that had not undergone the 'cut' was derisively referred to as *egesagane*. No boy wanted to remain *omosia*, the equivalent term for an uncircumcised male. As well, no girl wanted to remain *egesagane*. As such all boys looked forward to be circumcised to "become men" while girls longed to undergo clitoridectomy to "become women". This rite of passage was a major landmark in the lives of Abagusii.

Male Circumcision

Boys' circumcision (the actual removal of the foreskin) took place very early in the morning, in part to use the cold morning dew to numb the skin; a kind of anaesthesia (Nelson Nyang'era King'oina). A boy who successly went through the cut was no longer *omosia* (the uncircumcised), but *omomura* (a man). As the men (they must have undergone the ritual themselves) escorted the newly circumcised boy home following the 'surgery', they sung the song called *esimbore*. *Esimbore* is in several versions as you can see below. The various versions were sung to me by the late Julius Nyakwama Bosire of Bogiakumu Primary School, Bonchari, Dr. Evans Omosa Nyamwaka of Kisii University, Dr. Felix Orina Oyioka of Kibabii University and Professor John S. Akama of Kisii University. The different versions is as a result of the possibility of people living far apart from one another and also due to modification of the song by people of various localities. Here is the first version of *esimbore*.

Esimbore	Boys' Circumcision poem
Oyoo, oyoooo	This one this one, this one
Oyo-oo	This one
Oyoo, oyooo	This one this one, this one
Oyo-oo	This one

Obeire momura, obeire momura-a-a	Has become a man, has become a man
Oyo-oo	This one
Obeire momura, obeire momura-a-a-a	Has become a man, has become a man
Oyo-oo	This one
Arwane Sigisi na Botende-ee	To fight the Kipsigis and Kuria
Oyo-oo	This one
Arwane Sigisi na Botende-ee	To fight the Kipsigis and Kuria
Oyo-oo	This one
Ise Mokami oirire	Mokami's father has taken
Mboro chiaito	Our penises
Ise Mokami oirire	Mokami's father has taken
Mboro chiaito	Our penises
Ise Mokami oirire	Mokami's father has taken
Mboro chiaito	Our penises
Mboro chiaito-ii	Our penises-ii
Tiga aire mbororo	Let him take them. Anger
Bwamorire	Has filled him up!
Tiga aire mbororo	Let him take them. Anger
Bwamorire	Has filled him up!
Tiga aire mbororo	Let him take them. Anger
Bwamorire	Has filled him up!
Bwamorire-ii	Has filled him up-ii
Otureirwe itimo	For him a spear has been made
Na nguba imbibo-o-o-o	And a strong shield
Oyo-oo	This one
Otureirwe itimo	For him a spear has been made
Na nguba imbibo-o-o-o	And a strong shield
Oyo-oo	This one
Nchuo mwerorere enyamweri	Come and see a snake/python
Korwa engoro ime	From a cave (hole)
Nchuo mwerorere enyamweri	Come and see a snake/python
Korwa engoro ime	From a cave (hole)

Nchuo mwerorere enyamweri	Come and see a snake/python
Korwa engoro ime	From a cave (hole)
Korwa engoro ime-ii	From a cave (hole)-ii
Inchuo mwerore orokono	Come and see a bamboo
Rwekonoire	That has straightened itself
Inchuo mwerorere orokono	Come and see a bamboo
Rwekonoire	That has straightened itself
Inchuo mwerorere orokono	Come and see a bamboo
Rwekonoire	That has straightened itself
Rwekonoire-ii	That has straightened itself-ii
Nyanguba imbibo	One with astrong shield
Nyanguba imbibo-o-o	One with astrong shield
Oyo-oo	This one
Nyanguba imbibo	One with astrong shield
Nyanguba imbibe-o-o	One with astrong shield o-o
Oyo-oo	This one
Moisia moke teta	A lad who f**ks
Teta ng'ina	Let him copulate with his mother
Moisia moke teta	A lad who f**ks
Teta ng'ina-a-a-a	Let him copulate with his mother
Moisia moke teta	A lad who f**ks
Teta ng'ina	Let him f**k his mother
Teta ng'ina-ii	Let him copulate with his mother-ii
Aka embere ebasi	Iron your v*****
Mogoroba	In the evening
Aka embere ebasi	Iron your v*****
Mogoroba	In the evening
Aka embere ebasi	Iron your v*****
Mogoroba	In the evening
Mogoroba-ii	In the evening-ii
Omokungu kagotetwa	When a woman copulates
Igo agoseka	She smiles

Omokungu kagotetwa	When a woman copulates
Igo agoseka	She smiles
Omokungu kagotetwa	When a woman copulates
Igo agoseka	She smiles
Igo agoseka-ii	She smiles-ii

(Mr. Julius Bosire Nyakwama, Bogiakumu Primary School, Bogiakumu Location, Bonchari, 2007.

Oyo oyooo	He is here, he is here
Oyoo	He is
Oyo oyooo	He is here, he is here
Oyoo	He is
Omoisia nyakebororo	Small boy who has suffered pain
Bwakorire	Suffered pain
Omoisia nyakebororo	Small boy who has suffered pain
Bwakoriree	Suffered pain
Bwakoriree -- ee	Suffered pain --ee
Oyo oyoo	He is here, he is here
Oyoo	He is
Oyo oyoo	He is here, he is here
Oyoo	He is
Ise Mokami oirire	Mokami's father has taken
Mboro chiabo	Their penises
Ise Mokami oirire	Mokami's father has taken
Mboro chiaboo -- oo	Their penises
Nyanguba mbibo nyanguba mbibo-o-o	One to carry a thick war shield
Oyoo	This one
Nyanguba mbibo nyanguba mbibo-o-o	One to carry a thick war shield
Oyoo	This one
Omoisia omoke teta	Small lad, f**k
Teta nyoko	F**k your mother
Omoisia omoke teta	Small lad f**k
Teta nyoko - ee!	F**k your mother - ee

(Nelson King'oina Nyang'era:1999: 22-23).

Twachire Buya / We have arrived Well

Twachire Buya	We have arrived Well
Twachire buya twachire buya aa aa	We have come well we have come well aa aa
Bono mambia, bono mambia ee ee	This morning, this morning eeeh
Oyotarochi tiga ache - kwerorera	Whoever has never seen let him come
Kwerorera enyamweri - korwa engoro imee	To see for oneself a python from its hole
kwerorera enyamweri - korwa engoro imee	To see for oneself a python from its hole
kwerorera enyamweri - korwa engoro imee	To see for oneself a python from its hole
Korwa engoro imee.	from its hole.
Obeire 'momura, obeire 'momura aaa	He has become a man, he has become a man, aaa
Bono mambia, bono mambiaaa	This morning, this morning aaa
Ng'ina amosike, ng'ina amosikee	His mother to respect him, his mother to respect him eee
Tachi roche, tachi rocheee	Not to make him fetch water, not to make him fetch water, eee
Tachi kwaa, tachi kwaaa	Not to make him fetch vegetables, not to make him fetch vegetables, aaa
Oyo Oyoo - Oyoo.	This one - this one.

(Dr. Evans Nyamwaka of Kisii University. He collected the song from Nyamagesa village during male circumcision ceremony on 30/11/97).

According to Dr. Evans Nyamwaka, the 'python' in this circumcision song was meant to arouse in people the fear they had of the serpent. He says: "The penis was seen to be dangerous because it could break virginity in the event of having pre-marital sex. Virginity was expected to be respected and safe-guarded.

Oyo oyoo / Oyoo (This One)

Oyo oyoo	Oyoo (This One)
Oyo oyoo	He is here, he is here
Oyoo	He is
Obeire momura	He is now a man
Obeire momura eee	He is a man indeed

Oyo oyoo	He is here, he is here
Oyoo	He is
Oyo oyoo	He is here, he is here
Oyoo	He is
Omoisia nyakebororo	Boy you are hurting and seething with anger
Omoisia nyakebororo	Boy you are hurting and seething with anger
Oyo oyoo	He is here
Oyoo	He is
Oyo oyoo	He is here, he is here
Oyoo	He is
Totogia momura kieni	Never praise a man for his looks
Totogia momura kieni	Never praise a man for his looks
Motogie makora	But for his deeds
Motogie makora	But for his deeds
Oyoo	He is here
Oyo oyoo	He is here
Oyoo	He is here
Oyo oyoo	He is here, he is here
Oyoo	He is here
Ritimo riaye riatieriigwe	His spear has been sharpened
Tiga arwane Sigisi	Let him fight against the Kipsigis
Omoisia nyoko teta	Fearful boy you fuck your mother
Teta nyoko	Fuck your mother
Omoisia nyoko teta	Fearful boy, fuck your mother
Teta nyoko eee	Fuck your mother

(Orina: 2014)

Oyo! Oyo-o-o!	**Here he is! Here he is!**
Oyo-oyo-o-o!	Here he is!
Oyo-oyo-o-o!	Here he is!
Omoisia omoke mbororo bwamorire	(The circumcised) little boy is experiencing pain
Omoisia omoke ateta ng'ina	The little boy copulates with his mother!
Oyo-oyoo!	Here he is!
Oyo-oyoo!	Here he is!

Omoisia omoke mbororo bwamorire	(The circumcised) little boy has felt pain
Omoisia omoke ateta ng'ina	The little boy copulates with his mother!
Omoisia omoke ateta ng'ina	The little boy copulates with his mother!
Samokami[1] oirire 'mboro chiaito	Circumciser has taken our penises
Samokami oirire 'mboro chiaito	Circumciser has taken our penises
Tiga aire 'mbororo bwamorire	Let him take he is angry with us
Tiga aire 'mbororo bwamorire	Let him take he is angry with us
Oyotarochi tigache kwerorera	He who does not believe, let him come and witness
Oyotarochi tigache kwerorera	He who does not believe, let him come and witness
Kwerorera enyamweri ekorwa engoro ime	To witness the one like moonlight
Kwerorera enyamweri ekorwa engoro ime	Appearing from the cave/hole
Mboro chiaito indokore rwekonoire	Our penises are like a green tree
Mboro chiaito indokore rwekonoire	Our penises are like a green tree
Oyo-oyo-o-o! Oyoo!	Here he is!
Oyo-oyo-o-o! Oyoo!	Here he is!
Otureirwe itimo	He has been given a spear
Otureirwe itimo	He has been given a spear
Na nguba mbibo	And a big shield
Na nguba mbibo	And a big shield
Arwane Sigisi	Fight the Kipsigis
Arwane Sigisi	Fight the Kipsigis
Arwane Maasai	Fight the Maasai
Arwane Maasai	Fight the Maasai
Arwane Sugusu	Fight in the North
Arwane Sugusu	Fight in the North
Arwane Irianyi	Fight in the South

Arwane Irianyi	Fight in the South
Arwane Bobisa	Fight the enemy

(Akama:2017:51)

A Song for Esuguta

After circumcision, the boy was kept in a secluded hut. He was referred to as *omware,* the initiate and sometimes, pejoratively as *egesimba.* A special cubicle and bed were constructed for him using leaves and branches of *amabuko. Amabuko* plant had a sweet aroma or fragrance that supplied a sort of perfume in the house.

Three days after circumcision some men went out to cut *esuguta,* sod grass, and brought it to the house. The following *song of esuguta* was provided by Nelson Nyag'era King'oina (1999):

> Esabari nyasuguta abari
> Esabari nyasuguta abari
> Esabari rienyi
> Makomoke oremire 'nchera igoro
> Tiga areme mboremo bwaborire
> Yaya ee, yaya ee
>
> Eaoye tindi nyeni entata
> Esabari nyasuguta abari
> Makomoke oremire 'nchera igoro
> Tiga areme mboremo bwaborire
> Yaya ee, yaya ee.
>
> Bware bware bware
> Ese obororo bokorusia ng'ombe kiebo
> Esabari nyasuguta abari
> Makomoke oremire inchera igoro
> Tiga areme mboremo bwaborire
> Yaya ee, yaya ee.

Editor's note: *while the author has not provided a translation of the above song, the context can be gleaned from the foregoing one (by by Akama) and the following one from Oyioka*

The following is another version of *Song of Esuguta* that has been provided by Felix Orina Oyioka (2014:200). It goes as follows:

Esabari Nyasuguta	**The Journey of the Sod Grass**
Esabari Nyasuguta y'abare	The journey of the sod for initiates
Esabari Nyasuguta ya'bare esabari	The journey of the sod for initiates
Makomoke oremire 'nchera igoro	My aunt has ploughed the path
Eee tiga areme mboremo bwaborire	Let her, since she lacks land
Esabari Nyasuguta ya'bare	The journey of the sod for initiates
Ase obororo bokorusia ng'ombe kiebo	Where pain and anguish beget cows
Makomoke oremire 'nchera igoro	My aunt has ploughed the path
Eee tiga areme mboremo bwaborire	Let her, since she lacks land
Esabari Nyasuguta ya'bare	The journey of the sod for initiates
Esabari Nyasuguta ya'bare esabari	The journey of the sod for initiates
Esese endabu yaeta	A white dog has crossed
Mache ng'umbu	Over the ridge
Yarabirie ekemincha n'ekerenge	Its tail and feet glow

Another version of *Song of Esuguta* is given by John S. Akama (2017:57). The translation is also his. It goes as follows:

Esabarianyi y'esuguta	**Of initiates esuguta**
Esabarianyi y'esuguta y'abare esabarianyi	Of initiates *esuguta*
Aye, makamoke oremire inchera igoro	Oh, step-mother has cultivated on the main path
Ee, tiga areme 'mboremo bwamoborire	Yes, let her cultivate, she has no other garden
Aye, okwanigwe na'moeti na mogendi	Oh, she gets greetings from passers-by
Aye, okwanigwe nonde ataiitongo	Oh, she gets greetings from passers-by
Aye, okwanigwe na 'moeti na mogendi	Oh, she gets greetings from passers-by

The sod was planted in one of the corners of the house in which the circumcised boy lived. The plant was to be watered by the initiate daily. When he washed his hands he placed them above the *esuguta* so that the water dripped down on the plant. The growth and freshness of the grass signified that the evil spirits were kept at bay. According to Felix Orina Oyioka (2014) the sprouting of the grass "meant that the initiate would grow into a prosperous man".

It was a bad omen if the plant failed to sprout and grow. If the *esuguta* stopped growing or dried up and died, it was a sign that evil spirits had 'haunted' the boy and could spell doom to his future. To ward off these evil spirits (in the event of the grass dying), there had to be cleansing for the initiate. According to Nelson Nyang'era (1999), cleansing involved strangling an ewe and its blood shed.

The phrase used in the song *Makomoke oremire 'nchera igoro* (my aunt has ploughed the path) carries meaning. According to Orina (2014) it refers to the act of planting *esuguta* (sod) in the seclusion hut." He goes further to explain that:

> It is indeed bizarre as insinuated in the song but symbolised the initiate's agony concerning the life ahead. Once again, the initiate's life was depicted as a journey whose destination is uncertain, but through anguish, the initiate hoped to benefit from sacred grace and benevolence (40).

While Orina sees the phrase *Makomoke oremire 'nchera igoro* (my aunt has ploughed the path) as symbolizing the initiate's agony, others interpret the phrase to symbolize the cut foreskin of the penis. When the singers utter the words *Makomoke oremire nchera igoro* (my aunt has ploughed the path), they mean the circumciser has peeled off parts of the initiate's penis. Here *Makomoke* (Aunt) refers to the circumciser while *nchera igoro* (path) refers to the penis that has been dug (cut).

After the cut, according to Nelson King'oina Nyang'era, the boy stayed in seclusion for three moons and if he had healed arrangements were made for him to come out of seclusion. A night before the day of coming out, or a day of graduation, the boy was taken to his parents' house to talk to them for the first time since he went into seclusion. According to Nelson King'oina, the boy stood outside the parents' house and without seeing each other they talked as follows:

The Initiate: *Tata na baba borania* (father and mother query each other)

Parents: *Ee bana borania chiombe na abana. Gwassi Abanto na ng'ombe* (Yes, children query one another, cattle and children be blessed).

The boy got blessings from his parents. The following day, the day he came out of seclusion, the day of 'graduation', the initiate's head was shaved and he was fitted new clothes. On this day there would be plenty of food to eat and brew to partake. Neighbours would come to show kindness and unity. They would bring with them food, porridge and beer. One of the songs that were common on this occasion was *Ekiomogoko*. It was sung as follows:

Eki'Omogoko	**Selfish Woman**
Eki'omogoko n'omwana ogatoeire	What a selfish woman owns, we get it via the child
Eki'omogoko n'omwana ogatoeire	What a selfish woman owns, we get it via the child
Nosabwa rweni tokobirwa	You who cannot share your vegetables
N'omwana ogatoeire	We get it via the child
N'osabwa rweni tokobirwa	You who cannot share your vegetables
N'omwana ogatoeire	We get it via the child
Mogasamba keiririato	You ululate
Buna obairwe	As if given to you freely
Nyamaiyererio	The newly cut
Nyamasenyente	The newly cut
Eki'omogoko n'omwana ogatoeire	What a selfish woman owns, we get it via the child
Eki'omogoko n'omwana ogatoeire	What a selfish woman owns, we get it via the child
N'osabwa rweni tokobirwa	You who cannot share your vegetables
N'omwana ogatoeire	You ululate
N'osabwa rweni tokobirwa	You who cannot share your vegetables
N'omwana ogatoeire	
Mogasamba keiririato	You ululate
Buna obairwe	As if given to you freely

Nyamaiyererio	The newly cut
Nyamasenyente	The newly cut

There is another version of this song. It goes as follows:

Eki'omogoko	**Selfish Woman**
Eki'omogoko	What a selfish woman owns
N'omwana ogatoeire	We get it via the child
Ekiomogoko	What a selfish woman owns
N'omwana ogatoeire	We get it via the child
Nosabwa rweni tokobirwa	You who cannot share your vegetables
N'omwana ogatoeire	We get it via the child
Nosabwa rweni tokobirwa	What a selfish woman owns
N'omwana ogatoeire	We get it via the child
Mogasamba keiririato	You ululate
Buna obairwe	As if given to you freely
Nyamaiyererio	The newly cut
Nyamasenyente	The newly cut
Eki'omogoko	What a selfish woman owns
N'omwana ogatoeire	We get it via the child
Ekiomogoko	What a selfish woman owns
N'omwana ogatoeire	We get it via the child
Nosabwa rweni tokobirwa	You who cannot share your vegetables
N'omwana ogatoeire	We get it via the child
Nosabwa rweni tokobirwa	You who cannot share your vegetables
N'omwana ogatoeire	We get it via the child
Mogasamba keiririato	You ululate
Buna obairwe	As if given to you freely
Nyamaiyererio	The newly cut
Nyamasenyente	The newly cut
Ekiomogoko	What a selfish woman owns
N'omwana ogatoeire	We get it via the child
Eki'omogoko	What a selfish woman owns
N'omwana ogatoeire	We get it via the child
N'osabwa rweni tokobirwa	You who cannot share your vegetables

N'omwana ogatoeire	We get it via the child
N'osabwa rweni tokobirwa	You who cannot share your vegetables
N'omwana ogatoeire	We get it via the child
Mogasamba keiririato	You ululate
Buna obairwe	As if given to you freely
Nyamaiyererio	The newly cut
Nyamasenyente.	The newly cut

The song, *Ekiomogoko,* asserts that when a child (say) is circumcised, weds, etc. the selfish parent has no alternative but to feed the community.

On this day also the initiate's cubicle and bed which we earlier said was constructed of leaves and branches of *amabuko* (lavender) tree, was burnt by the boy's grandfather. During the burning of amabuko, men and big boys sung on top of their voices a song of burning amabuko, "Amabuko Abare."

Amabuko a 'Abare	**The Initiate's Amabuko**
Eeee amabuko abare eee ayire rero	Eee *amabuko* of the initiate eee is burnt today
Eeee amabuko abare eee abeire ribu	Eee *amabuko* of the initiate eee is burnt today
Eeee ayire rero eee tari rinde	Eee is burnt today eee not any other day
Eeee amabuko abare eee abeire ribu	Eee *amabuko* of the initiate eee has become ash
Eeee amabuko abare eee ayire rero	Eee *amabuko* of the initiate eee is burnt today
Eeee amabuko abare eee abeire ribu	Eee *amabuko* of the initiate has become ash
Eeee amabuko abare eee abeire ribu	Eee *amabuko* of the initiate has become ash
Eeee amabuko abare eee ayire rero	Eee *amabuko* of the initiate eee is burnt today
Eeee amabuko abare eee abeire ribu	Eee *amabuko* of the initiate has become ash

Eeee amabuko abare eee ayire rero   Eee *amabuko* of the initiate eee is burnt today

After the burning of *amabuko,* the boys were given a type of porridge called *ekenungu.* This was a fermented porridge which was sweetened through fermentation using yeast. Abagusii believed that the porridge supplied energy to the boys who had sung or were singing. The significance of the burning of *amabuko* was that the boy had now moved to another stage in life. He was now a man and not a lad. It was symbolic of burning one's childhood and taking on one's adulthood.

Female Circumcision

Female circumcision (a parallel inititation ceremony to male circumcision) was done using a small knife or a razor blade. Flour was sprinkled on the clitoris to aid the circumciser's grip, then the tip of the clitoris was cut. Girls usually lined up for the operation and once it was over for them all, the circumciser led in *ekeiririato,* ululation. And then later burst into a song called "Eaoye". "Eaoye" was collected by Christine Nyakerario Bundi and Felix Orina Oyioka

Eaoye

Eaoye Eaoye

Goko okorire buya

Orenge mokabaisia

Obeire mokabamura Arirriri

Atuta baba oyogoreirwe

Nche tingoreirie ndore motangi

Mosamba keiririato

Buna ogoreirwe

Nyamasenyente

Nyamaiyererio

 Arirriri

Eaoye eaoye

Esimbore yaito

Yarure rogoro

Rogoro ndwochabe

Eaoye Eaoye
Aririri
Atuta baba oyogoreirwe
Nche tingoreirie ndore motangi
Mosamba keiririato
Buna ogoreirwe
Nyamasenyente
Nyamaiyererio
Aririri

(Christine Nyakerario Bundi, 2018)

Editor's note: *while the author has not provided a translation of the above song, the context can be gleaned from the foregoing one .*

Eaye Oye	**Girls' Circumcision Song**
Eaye oye	Eaye oye
Goko okorire buya	The girl has done well
Eaye oye	Eaye oye
Orenge mokabaisia	Once a "wife" to little boys
Eaye oye	Eaye oye
Obeire mokabamura	Has become a wife of men
Eaye oye	Eaye oye
Gesare moka'Mbaka	Gesare-- Mbaka's wife
Eaye oye	Eaye oye
Oirire ebisono biaito	Has taken away our clitoris
Eaye oyee	Eaye oye
Ochire gotonga egete	To go and stick them on a stick.
Eaye oyee	Eaye oye
Omote ateba: "Gesare ominto"	Omete says: "My dear Gesare."
Eaye oye	Eaye oye
Omotwe ngong'ati ore	I am having headache
Eaye oye	Eaye oye
Mbate buya	Fondle me gently
Eaye oye	Eaye oye
Mbwate buya ngosamore	Fondle me gently I harvest you
Eaye oye	Eaye oye

Onsire buya onsire buya	Hold me up gently
Ngosamore	I harvest you
Eaye oye	Eaye oye
Ontate buya ontate buya	Caress me softly, caress me softly
Ngosamore	I harvest you
Aye oye	Eaye oye
Goko okorire buya	The girl has done well
Eaye oye	Eaye oye
Orenge mokabaisia	Once a girl friend to lads
Eaye oye	Eaye oye
Obeire mokamomura	Has become a girl-friend of men
Eaye oye	Eaye oye

(Christine Nyakerario Bundi, 2018)

Eaoye	**Eaoye**
Eaoye eaoye	Eaoye eaoye
Goko okorire buya	Be happy she has done well
Orenge mokabaisia	She was a wife of uncircumcised boys
Obeire mokabamura	Now she is a wife of circumcised men
Eaoye eaoye	Eaoye eaoye
Eaoye eaoye	Eaoye eaoye
Esimbore yaito	Our men's song
Yarure sugusu	Has come from the North
Eaoye eaoye	Eaoye eaoye
Eaoye eaoye	Eaoye eaoye
Sugusu Ndwochabe	The North of Ochabe (name of a man)
Irianyi neyaito	The South is ours
Totogia moiseke kieni	Never praise her for her beauty
Motogie mwana	But for bearing a child
Eaoye eaoye	Eaoye eaoye

(Orina: 2014)

The song comprises of *amang'ana ansoni,* taboo words. The song says that the girl has become the "wife" of *abamura,* the circumcised boys/men, and is no longer the "wife" of *abaisia,* the uncircumcised lads. The song aims at encouraging other girls to go in for the cut.

The song mocks the parents of the initiated girl. It decribes the parents' love affairs when in bed: *Mbate buya, mbate buya* (fondle me gently, fondle me gently) *Ontate buya, ontate buya* (caress me gently, caresss me gently) *Ngosamore* (I harvest you, meaning "I sex with you."). The song dwells on the obscenity describing the initiated parents' love affairs, sex, clitoris and the cutting act. The parent, listening to the song, responds with smiles and joy. No one gets embarrassed or offended by what the song says as it is an occasion when such indecent songs are accepted.

According to Dr. Matunda Nyanchama, the indescence in the song had a purpose. It was the only occasion such indescence was accepted. The poetry was not accepted outside the context of circumcision, for then it would be considered indescent and taboo. According to him, the indecence was meant to help people to 'unwind'. People, having done work throughout the year, been descent all along and occupied themselves with building the community, they needed a moment of rest and a moment of 'bursting out', in which they threw all cares to the air. It was an occasion in which they reflected back to the year of hard work, a future that was ahead and how to bring fulfillment to life. They had to 'unwind', 'exhale' and 'let it go' after a whole year of involvement and occupation, after a period of carefully behaving well, avoiding taboo words and actions.

During circumcision, any obscene word was dressed in a figurative language which would be comprehended by the elders and those with wisdom. (Oyo oyo oo. Samokami oirire, chimori chiabo, Samokami oirie, chimori chiabo. Tiga aire mbororo bwamorire). The 'chimori' was a pun on 'chimbooro'. Another example is 'imbwate buya ingosamore'. The woman is calling upon the man to hold her tightly so that she gives him the best during sex. This kind of revelation helped the naive and shy couples to feel free hence arousal into renewal of their sex life.

The freedom to expresss themselves through such obscenity, at the same time, was intended to show that sex and romance was not a taboo. The words of the song are in praise of sex, e.g. "omokungu ekero agotetwa nigo agoseka". This was meant to establish some kind of rapporteur among men and women so that they would all feel at ease even during coitus. At the same time, this was a deliberate attempt to educate the young on romance and sex.

In the following female circumcision song, *Gwakunire enkuna* the chameleon symbolizes the clitoris.

Gwakunire Enkuna	**You have Touched the (Un)Touchable**
Gwakunire enkuna--kuna!	You have touched, oh touch!
Gwakunire enkuna--kuna!	You have touched, oh touch!
Kuna Moyare, ee baba kuna	Touch ee – touch!
Nakunire enkuna – kuna!	I have touched - a touch!
Nakunire enyambu – kuna!	I have touched a chameleon – touch!
Nakunire enyambu	I have touched a chameleon – touch!
Kuna moyare, ee baba kuna!	Touch ee touch!
Kuna onkuneranie – kuna!	Touch and touch for me – touch!
Kuna onkuneranie – kuna!	Touch and touch for me – ee!
Kuna moyare ee, baba kuna!	Oh touch!

According to Dr. Evans Nyamwaka, Abagusii reference to the chameleon at this period was mainly from the perspective of colour. A chameleon changes its colour now and again. It cannot be noticed easily in any particular environment. The connotation given in reference to the clitoris as a chameleon was that of being 'sacred'. 'Sacred' because its feelings were prone to change from excitement during copulation and pains at birth. This song was developed to caution the initiates to abstain from pre-marital, 'free' or 'unholy' sex. The songs reminded the initiates to preserve the Abagusii culture and customs which condemned sex before marriage. Any girl, according to Abagusii custom, who had sex before marriage was considered an outcast.

In the case where a girl does not successfully go through the cut, e.g. she happens to scream during the operation, the mockery song, *enkuri,* was sung for her.

Enkuri	**The Screamer**
E Nyangomba,	Ee the screamer, the screamer
E Nyangomba	Ee the screamer, the screamer
Enyangomba	Ee the screamer, the screamer
Orogondo	
Otumire otumire	She has jumped, jumped
Otumire 'getumo	She has jumped, jumped
Ocharara ocharara	She has pranced, pranced
Ocharara n'omoyio	She has pranced with a knife
E n'omoyio e n'omoyio	A knife, a knife
N'omoyio obirende	A knife of the initiation trough
N'Obonyo n'Obonyo	
N'Obonyo bw'Okondo	
Ocharara ocharara	She has pranced, pranced
Ocharara n'omoyio	She has pranced with a knife
N'omoyio n'omoyio	A knife, a knife
N'omiyio obirende	A knife of the initiation trough

The song mocks her for soiling the trough, the initiating stool, on which she sits when being cut. In such an instance, a bad circumciser will curse her by saying *aye okoria abasacha na abana okore* (you will devour all your husbands and children), meaning: she will have her husband and children die when she gets married. The circumciser hits the screaming girl with the hilt of her circumcising knife as she utters these words. According to Nelson King'oina, this curse worked in the community and, therefore, girls were encouraged to be brave when they were cut to avoid the curse.

To ward off the curse of the circumciser, the parents of the girl provided her (circumciser) with a ewe. This was slaughtered to cleanse *orotuba,* the circumciser's trough.

According to Mr. Nelson Nyang'era, such a girl who had cursed the circumciser's trough was not sponsored or godmothered. She was not led into the house by a godmother, but by a ewe which is slaughtered in order to cleanse her of the evil spirits. The belief was that if she was not cleased, she will be haunted by the devil all the way into the future. Her children and husband(s) would die.

The following song was sung by a girl who had successfully gone through female initiation and had hence become a "woman" in the Abagusii tradition.

Ngaremia Oyonde	**I Inspired a Friend**
Inche mokarikere	I the brave
Nachiete orotuba	Was circumcised
Ngaremia oyonde ominto, ah!	I inspired my friend, ah
Esibie ogende	Wash and go
Ogende ogende	Go and go
Orokarema sinsi, eeh!	Didn't move hips at all
Chietunda kere	Me Chietunda kere
Chietunda kere	Me Chietunda kere
Nchitache	I walked bravely
Naende nsikini, aa!	Through the ritual fires
Esibie ogende	Wash and go
Ogende ogende	Go and go
O karema sinsi, ee!	I was brave, ee!
Obonyo bw'Ombongi	Obonyo daughter of Ombongi
Ochiete rotuba	Who was being circumcised
Akabuga ng'a uui!	Screamed uui!
Kiki kiki kioreka nda.	Kiki kiki, she a coward

This poem is sung by a newly-initiated girl who recalls the time she was circumcised. In the song she recalls that she bravely walked through the ritual fires, and with pride. Because she did not scream during the operation, her action inspired a friend who was next in the line. She also says about a girl, Obonyo daughter of Ombongi, who screamed "uui!" when being cut. She terms her a coward in the poem.

A girl who successfully went through the operation was

kept in seclusion. Within three days of the operation while in seclusion, the godmother and some women went for special grass, *esuguta,* cut it and brought it to the house where the circumcised girl lived. It was planted in one of the corners of the seclusion house. She had to water this special grass, *esuguta,* as long as she was in seclusion, thus keeping it alive and green. It was not allowed to dry while she was in seclusion. The grass symbolised her life, which was to be kept watered. As with the case of boys, if the grass dried off, it was deemed a curse and an elaborate cleansing ceremony had to be done to evade potential effects of the curse. The song for this occasion of *esuguta* was like that one for the boys.

Chapter 4
Poetry for Marriage Ceremonies

Poems were sung before, during and after marriage ceremonies. It started with courtship, between the girl and the boy, assisted by a go-between, *esigani*. This was followed by a number of activities that led to consent to the marriage by parties which was followed by payment of dowry. And finally came the marriage ceremony. In all these, poetry coloured the events and played a crucial role in the communication of taboo words, information and precepts to the bride and the groom, parents, relatives and the entire community. Poetry provided entertainment and enhanced harmony, love and peace among the people during this occasion.

Mzee Nelson Nyang'era and Nemwel Mogere Atemba both recall that members of one clan were not allowed to marry. These were considered "family" as they had the same ancestry. *Esigani*, the go-between who acted as a bridge between the two families of different clans, ensured that intermarriage among the members of the same clan did not take place. This was to curb the dangers that came with inbreeding[1].

1. Before Courtship

As a boy and girl grew up in the Abagusii community, people looked forward to seeing them marry and have children. Nothing else was more important than getting the right man or woman to marry and raise a family. As alluded to in earlier sections, children were at the core of perpetuation of the community into future generations.

In some cases parents became anxious and over-possessed about the marriage of their sons and daughters, especially where the children's peers may have been coupled already. Such parents went to the extent of being practically involved

---

1 **Editor's Note:** *Nelson King'oina Nyang'era and John Akama have dealt with this extensively in their respective books. (see bilbliography).*

in influencing their children's thoughts and feelings with respect to the choice of their mates.

For a boy, his mother would be heard sighing and saying: *Nyansarora okuma Bonyando, ng'ai ngochia nyakiore amotimie getinge gose boiko bware gocha ang'e* (There is a girl called Nyansarora at Bonyando clan reputed for her character; I wish my son could marry her). Nyansarora was an imaginary girl who was reputed for her character. Every mother wished her son could marry a well-behaved girl like her.

Enyabarati ya Baba

In this poem, "Enyabarati Ya Baba," the boy is referred to as the "mother's cow". The cow is asked to moo when other cows moo. He should do what other cows do or have done. The meaning of this is that he should marry as other boys have done or are doing. In the last two lines of this poem the boy is told thus: *Aye baba tari na'motenyerinko* (you! mother has no one to fetch firewood for her). Women were married to help with such chores (among many others) as collecting firewood and helping cook for their mothers-in-law. The boy, therefore, is being asked to marry to let her mother have a daughter-in-law who would help with firewood collection. This song, therefore, is an encouragement for the boy to marry. Let us sing the song together:

Enyabarati ya Baba	**My Mother's Cow**
Enyabarati ya baba	My mother's cow
Echinde chikwana	When others moo
Na'aye kwana	You should also moo
Enyabarati ya baba	My mother's cow
Echinde chikwana	When others moo
Na'aye kwana	You should also moo
Aye baba tari	Mother has no one
Namotenyerinko	To gather firewood for her.
Aye baba tari	Mother has no one
Namotenyerinko	To gather firewood for her.

Enyabarati ya baba	My mother's cow
Echinde chikwana	When others moo
Na'aye kwana	You should also moo
Aye baba tari	Mother has no one
Namotenyerinko	To gather firewood for her.
Aye baba tari	Mother has no one
Namotenyerinko	To gather firewood for her.
Aye baba tari	Mother has no one
Namotenyerinko	To gather firewood for her.
Aye baba tari	Mother has no one
Namotenyerinko	To gather firewood for her.

Kemwa Geteneine

Girls were moulded to behave well so as to get good husbands to marry them. Otherwise *Omoiseke omobe 'momura oare aganyete* (a bad girl awaits a distant suitor to marry her) (Okemwa: 2012). The girl who was of poor character would only be married by someone from far away; someone who possibly does not know of her bad character.

Boys were enticed by the proverb, *kaya 'nkaya kanga Mwango o'Matara* (as beautiful as Mwango, daughter of Matara) (Okemwa:2012). Legend has it that Mwango, daughter of Matara, was once the most beautiful girl in Gusii. She was small in stature but very charming and industrious -- a role model. So girls were encouraged to behave like her so as to attract boys to marry them.

Ribina was one of the occasions in the Abagusii calendar that played a big role in enticing both boys and girls to marry. *Ribina* ceremonies took place during droughts and were used to beseech *Engoro* (God) to bring rain. Around mid day on the ribina day, recalls Mzee Nemwel Mogere Atemba (7/03/2009), a whistle was blown to call all people to *ogotuma ribina ekegoro igoro* (to jump ribina on top of a hill). People assembled on top of the hill. *Omonyibi,* the priest was expected to arrive at around four o'clock to lead the prayers. Between mid day and four oclock, there were curtain-raisers, young girls who could be jumping waiting for the priest to come. Only women participated in *ogotuma ribina*. Men were not allowed to participate in the dancing since it was believed that only women's cry and prayers could readily be received by *Engoro*, God. As young girls curtain-raised by jumping *ribina*, men could watch the dances from afar and sometimes also engaged in inter-clan wrestling activities.

The girls normally had no bras to cover their breasts. Boys would stand at a distance watching them dance the *ribina* dance. They would lust as they stared at the girls shaking their breasts and bare stomachs. The young girls were aware of the heat of lust they caused in the boys. One of the poems that explain the experience during that occasion was "Kemwa geteneine."

Kemwa Geteneine	**Breasts Standing**
Kemwa geteneine	A firm breast
Omoiseke kemwa geteneine	A girl with a firm breast
Kemwa geteneine	A firm breast
Omoiseke kemwa geteneine	A girl with a firm breast
Aye otanyorokia enchera 'nchie mwabo	Show me the way to her home
Aye otanyorokia enchera 'nchie mwabo	Show me the way to her home
Eekemwa geteneine	A firm breast
Omoiseke kemwa geteneine	A girl with a firm breast
Yatenenia orogondo	It swells its nape
Eturwa yatenenia orogondo	A bull swells its nape
Yatenenia orogondo	It swells its nape
Eturwa yatenenia orogondo	A bull swells its nape
Buna ekaroche eng'era sokobe	As if he has seen she-cow afar
Buna ekaroche eng'era sokobe	As if he has seen she-cow afar
Yatenenia orogondo	It swells its nape
Eturwa yatenenia orogondo	A bull swells its nape

Abera riberera	It melts in the heat
Amaguta abera riberera	Oil melts in the heat
Abera riberera	It melts in the heat
Amaguta abera riberera	Oil melts in the heat
Otakoyabeka ase akendu	Put it in a cool place
Otakoyabeka ase akendu	Put it in a cool place
Abera riberera	It melts in the heat
Amaguta abera riberera	Oil melts in the heat
Tuma ango ekegirango	Jump up like Abagirango do
Abaito tuma ngo ekegirango	
Tuma ango ekegirango	Jump up like Abagirango do
Abaito tuma ngo ekegirango	Our girls, jump up like Abagirango do
Abaiseke amagoti asogote	Girls lie down
Abaiseke amagoti asogote	Girls lie down
Tuma ango ekegirango	Jump up like Abagirango do
Abaito tuma ngo ekegirango	Our girls, jump up like Abagirango do

The girls' display ignited desire in the boys, thus encouraging them to marry. According to Mzee Samwel Ombasa Tamaro, girls and boys desired one another and sought for opportunities, not only during *ribina* occasions, to marry and have children. However, *Ribina's* preliminary activities – *ribina* dance by girls and inter-clan wrestling -- provided an enormous opportunity for girls and boys to seduce one another and arrange for marriage.

After the young girls had had their time, *omonyibi*, the priest arrived at four in what could be described as the most spectale moment. Old women, *abang'ina bonsi* (sing. *Omong'ina bwensi*), who were past the age of menopause, assembled, clad in their *chingoba* (skin-clothes), ready for the jumping. *Ribina* was majorly for these old women. They jumped as they sung a series of songs that beseeched *Engoro*, God, to bring rain. Mzee Nemwel Atemba recalls one of the songs sung during the jumping (8/03/2019):

Nare kua ching'eni	I was looking for vegetable
Eee oyaye	Eee oyaye
Omoinati one ogerire	My husband is the cause
Kagonsaba ching'eni	He asks for vegetable
Oo oyaye	Oo oyaye
Buna ndege eboire	Like a bell that is tied to something
Nare kua ching'eni	I was looking for vegetable
Eee oyaye	Eee oyaye
Omoinati one ogerire	My husband is the cause
Kagonsaba ching'eni	He asks for vegetable
Oo oyaye	Oo oyaye
Buna ndege eboire	Like a bell that is tied to something

(Nemwel Mogere Atemba, 8/03/2019)

The above song refers to a drought when greens dry up and vegetable is scarce. In the song a woman is lamenting. She says that her husband mumbles and complains about vegetables. She equates his noise and complaints to a bell that is tied to something and keeps on ringing. This is an example of the songs that the old women sung as they desperately jumped up, cried and sweated as the priest prayed and called for rain.

It is said that after the *ribina* dance was over, it rained cats and dogs on the third day.

As we have noted *ribina* occasion provided an overwhelming opportunity for courtship among boys and girls. However, Mzee Samwel Ombasa Tamaro says that there were other meeting outlets for boys and girls. For instance, he talks about a place called Tabaka where there was tall smooth grass. In this place, groups of girls met from time to time and whipped off their *chingoba* (hides that were used as clothes) and strolled naked in the tall grass. Those days, Tamaro states, men respected the women and could not sexually harass them, unlike today when we hear cases of rape and molestation. As young men passed by, they stared at the girls' nudity, something that sparked desire in them. The following song, sang by Samwel

Tamaro, was sung in praise of the girls' extraordinary courage to walk naked and expose their beautiful bodies.

Egetii Gia'Tabaka	**At Tabaka Open Field**
Egetii gia'Tabaka	In the open field of Tabaka
Omoiseke atara getirianda	A girl walks about naked
Egetii gia'Tabaka	In the open field of Tabaka
Omoiseke atara getirianda	A girl walks about naked
Atare gotara nangoba e!	Oh, couldn't she clad herself in *engoba*, e!
Atare gotara nangoba e!	Oh, couldn't she clad herself in *engoba*, e!
Atare gotara nangoba e!	Oh, couldn't she clad herself in *engoba*, e!
Atare gotara nangoba e!	Oh, couldn't she clad herself in *engoba*, e!
Egetii gia'Tabaka	In the open field of Tabaka
Omoiseke atara getirianda	A girl walks about naked
Egetii gia'Tabaka	In the open field of Tabaka
Omoiseke atara getirianda	A girl walks about naked
Atare gotara nangoba e!	Oh, couldn't she clad herself in *engoba*, e!
Atare gotara nangoba e!	Oh, couldn't she clad herself in *engoba*, e!
Atare gotara nangoba e!	Oh, couldn't she clad herself in *engoba*, e!
Atare gotara nangoba eeeeee	Oh, couldn't she clad herself in *engoba*, e!

Tata Omboreire Rara Saiga

As mentioned earlier, rape or molestation of women was unheard of in the Abagusii community. Women and girls were given due respect and held in high esteem. Boys lusted for the girls, but customs and traditions prohibited them from any indecent acts. However, folklore has it that, once upon a time in the community, there was a boy who could not overcome his lust for his sister. He raped her! The oddity of the case found itself in a song. The song sung by the victim--his sister--is a cry and a shocking revelation. She says that she didn't believe that her own brother, Ogembo, could rape her.

Tata Omboreire Rara Saiga	**Father, he has asked to sleep in his hut!**
Omboreire rara saiga	Father told me to spend a night in the hut
Tata omboreire rara saiga	Father told me to spend a night in the hut
Omboreire rara saiga	Father told me to spend a night in the hut
Tata omboreire rara saiga	Father told me to spend a night in the hut
Nakagete Ogembo n'oyominto	I thought Ogembo was my brother
Nakagete Ogembo n'oyominto	I thought Ogembo was my brother
Nakagete Ogembo n'oyominto	I thought Ogembo was my brother
Nakagete Ogembo n'oyominto	I thought Ogembo was my brother
Omboreire rara saiga	Father told me to spend a night in the hut
Tata omboreire rara saiga	Father told me to spend a night in the hut
Omboreire rara saiga	Father told me to spend a night in the hut
Tata omboreire rara saiga	Father told me to spend a night in the hut
Nakagete Ogembo n'oyominto	I thought Ogembo was my brother
Nakagete Ogembo n'oyominto	I thought Ogembo was my brother
Nakagete Ogembo n'oyominto	I thought Ogembo was my brother
Nakagete Ogembo n'oyominto	I thought Ogembo was my brother

Omoiseke Omomwamu

In the Abagusii community we had light and dark skinned girls. There are various perceptions men and the community attached to them. For instance, a girl of light complexion was preferred to a girl with a dark complexion. This is because the one of light complexion was thought to be more beautiful than the other. The following song confirms this:

Omoiseke Omomwamu	**A Girl of Dark Complexion**
Noba 'kieni aye togotebwa	The dark one
Aye omoiseke omomwamu	Even if beautiful no one praises you
Noba 'kieni aye togotebwa	You girl of dark complexion

Ayi n'esang'onde ekona gotebwa	Oh, only one of light complexion is praised
Ayi n'esang'onde ekona gotebwa	Oh, only one of light complexion is praised
Aye omoiseke omomwamu	You girl of dark complexion
Noba 'kieni aye togotebwa	Even if beautiful no one praises you
N'esang'onde ekona gotebwa	Only one of light complexion is praised
Ekona gotebwa ee baba	Is praised, ee, ee
N'esang'onde ekona gotebwa ee baba	Only one of light complexion is praised, ee
N'esang'onde ekona gotebwa	Only one of light complexion is praised

This poem tells a girl with a skin of dark complexion that no matter how beautiful she is, no one is going to sing a song in praise of her. Instead, a song will be sung in praise of the girl of light complexion. The poem seems to praise and appreciate the light-skinned girls.

Omoiseke Omomwamu

While "Omoiseke Omomwamu" praises girls of light complexion, another song of similar title approves girls of dark complexion, holding true the adage that "beauty is in the eyes of the beholder". The song praises a girl of dark complexion, and with huge thighs. The song says that a girl of dark complexion has stunned a boy with her huge thighs. As she walks up the hill of Manga, the boy is watching her huge thighs. This poem is telling girls of dark complexion that they are beautiful and have secret admirers out there.

Omoiseke Omomwamu	**Girl of Dark Complexion**
Omoiseke omomwamu	Girl with a dark complexion
Nyakebwato	With big thighs
Ogotira Manga	Going up the Manga hill
Omonyene eng'ombe	The one with dowry
Namoroche.	Is watching you
Omoiseke omomwamu	Girl with a dark complexion
Nyakebwato	With big thighs

Ogotira Manga	Going up the Manga hill
Omonyene eng'ombe	The one with dowry
Namoroche.	Is watching you
Ee namoroche, ee baba	Is watching you, ee, baba
Omonyene eng'ombe namoroche, ee baba	The one to pay dowry is watching you, ee baba
Omonyene eng'ombe namoroche	The one to pay dowry is watching you, ee baba

Obomwamu

As with the previous poem, the following one puts more emphasy on girls of dark complexion. The poem says that the dark skin is beautiful as it doesn't need oil to shine. Those girls who are dark should not wish they were of light skin.

Obomwamu	**Dark Skin**
Obomwamu 'mbore obuya	A dark skin is beautiful
Ee baba ominto	Ee, oh, my
Obomwamu sirikiani	Dark complexion
Ee oyonde	Ee, oh
Bichaga bigotogia	Attracts praises
Ee baba ominto	Ee, oh my
Obomwamu 'mbore obuya	Dark skin is beautiful
Ee baba ominto	Ee, oh my
Botakari 'maguta	A skin that doesn't need oil
Ee oyonde ominto	Eee, oh my
Obomwamu obosera	The dark skin that's swarthy
Ee baba ominto	Ee, ooh.

'Moiseke Nyakieni Kebariri

This song condemns girls of light complexion. The poem says that the girl with light complexion should take her beauty to Bobaracho. Bobaracho was a popular market in Gusii where boys and girls used to meet for courtship. A girl, who was known to have poor character, will go there and get a boy from far away who will court her. The boy, having no knowledge about her bad character, will marry her. Abagusii's proverb *omoiseke omobe 'momura o'are aganyete* (a bad girl awaits a distant boy to marry her) (Okemwa: 2012) comes true in this situation.

Bobaracho is where the biggest market was. So, any ill-cultured lady, even though of brown complexion, would resort, out of pride, to parade her beauty at the market and in most cases become promiscuous. And so, the elders are worried that in the event that such a thing happens, then boys will have nowhere to walk to. In other words, they will have no one to marry. She becomes a beauty wasted.

'Moiseke Nyakieni Kebariri	**The Girl with a Light Complexion**
'Moiseke nyakieni kebariri	A girl with light complexion
Aire ekieni Bobaracho	To take her beauty to Bobaracho
'Moiseke nyakieni kebariri	A girl with light complexion
Aire ekieni Bobaracho	To take her beauty to Bobaracho
Aire ekieni Bobaracho	Take her beauty to Bobaracho
Nario abamura baramwanche	Where boys will admire her
Aire ekieni Bobaracho	Take her beauty to Bobaracho
Nario abamura baramwanche	Where boys will admire her
Omong'ina arera boira	Mother cries everyday
Nyakieni kenga mache	Her beauty is like water
Nyakieni kebariri	The girl with a light complexion
Nyakieni kenga mache	Her beauty is like water.

Nyabeta

While the boys and girls grew, they were not allowed to engage in sex, or in immoral activites. It was a taboo! The proverb *mosae kengera 'mbusuro chiao, tichitaroka, chirusie bagaka kenuso mioro,* tells a young man to "guard his seeds lest they explode and, in the process, remove tobacco from the elders' nostrils". This is a warning to the youth to control their sexual desires to avoid causing unnecessary worries to elders who are supposed to be relaxed sniffing their tobacco. The proverb is meant to warn boys not to impregnant girls.

In traditional Abagusii society, girls were safeguarded from immoral activities. They were kept away from situations which could make them vulnerable to boys and tempt them to have sex. In traditional Abagusii community it was unheard of for a girl to become pregnant when she was not married. As indicated previously, it was also a taboo to make love with a girl or boy who came from one's clan. The boys were warned with the following proverb: *mwana tochega mino o'Nyakoni neba 'nene* (my son don't 'stir' within your own clan, regardless of how big it is regarded to be). In this proverb, the boy is warned not to stir things (do sex) within his own clan, no matter how far the clan spreads.

If a boy impregnated a girl from his clan and she became married later on, the boy would not drink milk of any of the cows paid as dowry to the girl's home.

The first girl to become pregnant in the Abagusii community is deemed to be Nyabeta, daughter of Orego. A poem was composed for her and is sung unto these days to girls who happen to become pregnant before marriage.

Nyabeta	**Nyabeta**
Nyabeta ore bw'Orego, ee!	Nyabeta, daughter of Orego, ee
Nyabeta ore bw'Orego	Nyabeta, daughter of Orego, ee
Nyagetundi kere nda	With a thing pounding in her belly
Egetundi kere inda, ee!	A thing pounding in her belly, ee
Ee, Nyagetundi kere nda	Ee, a thing pounding in her
Egekonya komotunda	It pounds in her
Egekonya komotunda eee	It pounds in her, ee!
Egekona komotunda	It shakes in her
Buna amabere amayio	Like fresh milk
Kai kwarusia enda eyio, eee	Where did you get that pregnancy from?
Ekai kwarusia enda eyio	Where did you get that pregnancy from?
Enarusia amatoke ime	I got it in the banana plantation
Ng'aki oraibore oroke?	What name will you give it?
Ng'aki oraibore oroke?	What name will you give it?
Oibore oroke Matoke.	Name it Bananas.

The poem is sad and satirical. It is asking the girl the following questions: Where did you get that pregnancy from? What name will you call the child when it is born? Of course, she won't be allowed to give a clan's name to her born child since she doesn't belong to that clan. So, the poem asks her: "What name will you give the child?" The poem concludes by telling her to name her child *Matoke* (bananas) since it is only in the banana plantation that is believed to be a place where illicit love affairs, assumably like hers, could take place.

Girls and boys were supposed to behave well. They were to rise to the expectation of the community.

Richuto

As we have said earlier, boys and girls were under pressure to marry when they came of age. It was very sad for a boy who could not marry because he was impotent. He had no value if he could not marry and have children. Children were the pride of the family and the community. Those who delayed their marriage because of impotence were ridiculed by the song, "Richuto."

Richuto	**The Impotent One**
Ee, ndire o'Michieka richuto	Ee, there is at Michieka's an impotent one.
Baba-a-a, richuto ndire o'Michieka ee	Baba-a-a, an impotent one at Michieka's, e
Ndire o'Michieka richuto	There is at Michieka's an impotent one
Ee, richuto, eee, ee	Ee, an impotent one, eee, ee
E kayi oranyuome richuto?	Ee, where will you marry from, you impotent one?
Baba-a-a richuto kayi oranyuome? Ee	Baba-a-a, the impotent one where will you marry from?
E kayi oranyuome richuto?	E, where will you marry from?
Ee richuto, eee, ee	Ee, the impotent one, eee, ee
Ee, ritube eng'ondi	Ee, cover him with a goat-skin
Tindirora	So that I don't see him
Baba-a-a tindirora, e ritube eng'ondi, ee	Baba-a-a, so that I don't see him, cover him with a goat-skin
Ee, ritube eng'ondi	Ee, cover him with a goat-skin
Tindirora	So that I don't see him
EE tindirora, eee, ee	Ee, so that I don't see him, eee, ee

Oral Poetry in Africa

Motube esike ya'bweri	Cover him with dung from cow-shed
Ee ya'bweri, motube esike	E, cow-shed, cover him with dung
Motube esike ya'bweri	Cover him with dung from cow-shed
Ee ya'bweri, eee	Ee, of cow-shed,
Ya bweri	Of cow-shed
Ndire ng'umbu eria risabara	Beyond the river there is an impotent one
Baba-a-a risabara ndire ng'umbu eria, ee	Baba-a-a, the impotent one is beyond the river yonder, e
Ndire ng'umbu eria risabara	Beyond the river there is an impotent one
Ya bweri	The impotent one
Motube eng'ondi timorora	Cover him with dung from cow-shed
Baba-a-a timorora, motube eng'ondi, e	E, cow-shed, cover him with dung
Motube eng'ondi timorora	Ee, of cow-shed,
E timorora, eee, ee	Of cow-shed
Ning'o oranyuome risabara?	Who will marry the impotent?
Baba-a-a risabara ning'o oranyuome? Ee	Baba-a-a, the impotent one, who will marry, e
Ning'o oranyuome risabara	Who will marry the impotent one?
Risabara, eee, ee	The impotent one, eee, ee
Motube esike ya'bweri	Cover him with dung from cow-shed
E ya'bweri, motube esike, e	E, cow-shed, cover him with dung
Motube esike ya'bweri	Ee, of cow-shed,
E yabweri, eee, ee	Of cow-shed

Bw'enkororo Amiyende

While the last poem expressed some sympathy for an impotent man, *Bw'enkororo Amiyende* praised a boy who had great virtues. This is a boy who did everything according to the community's expectations. The son of Miyende was strong, kind, helpful and generous.

Bw'enkororo Amiyende	**The Warrior of Miyende**
E bw'enkororo amiyende	The warrior of Miyende
Bw'enkororo amiyende-ee	The warrior of Miyende

E bw'enkororo amiyende	The warrior of Miyende
Bw'enkororo amiyende-ee	The warrior of Miyende
Ee naigwa ingokarariere-eee	Ee, I have heard your foot-stamping
Ee naigwa ingokarariere-eee	Ee, I have heard your foot-stamping
Buna ndege aboire	As if encircled with bangle anklets
Bwenkororo amiyende	The warrior of Miyende
Bwenkororo amiyeeende	The warrior of Miyende
Bwenkororo amiyende	The warrior of Miyende
Bwenkororo amiyeeende	The warrior of Miyende
Ee naigwa ingokarariere-eee	Ee, I have heard your foot-stamping
Ee naigwa ingokarariere-eee	Ee, I have heard your foot-stamping
Buna ndege aboire	As if encircled with bangle anklets

Poetry of Courtship

Having explored life as it was before courtship, let us now move on and examine experiences of a girl and a boy when both reached the ripe age of marriage. Girls and boys, who had reached such an age, received intense pressure from the community to marry. This pressure is indicated in the *omoino* (clasical poem) "Tata Matanga Chiombe," contributed by Samwel Ombasa Tamaro (2017)

Tata Matanga Chiombe

This *omoino* was sung by an old man or men. It was a response to a girl who complained that her brothers had refused to marry so that their father could be relieved from the task of tending for his cows. If these brothers married, their father's cows would be paid as dowry to their newly-married wives, hence the (father) would be relieved of the task of having to take care of them. In addition to having no cows to bother him (father), he would have daughters-in-law who would support him in his old age.

Tata Matanga Chiombe	**For Father to Look After Cows**
Eee tata matang'a chiombe-ee	For father to look after cows
E tata na'bamura atabwati	Does it mean he doesn't have boys?

Eee tata matang'a chiombe-ee	For father to look after cows
E tata na'bamura atabwati	Does it mean he doesn't have boys?
Ee tata n'abamura atabwati	Ee, doesn't father have boys?
Abamura'gesera kenga nsembe	Boys who are handsome?
Ee tata n'abamura atabwati	Handsome boys, handsome boys
Abamura 'gesera kenga nsembe	Boys who are handsome
Kenga'nsembe	Handsome
Abamura'gesera kenga 'nsembe	Boys who are handsome
Kenga'nsembe	Handsome
Abamura gesera kenga 'nsembe-eee	Boys who are handsome
Eee tata matang'a chiombe-ee	For father to look after cows
E, tata na'bamura atabwati	Does it mean he doesn't have boys?
Eee tata matang'a chiombe-eee	For father to look after cows
E tata na'bamura atabwati	Does it mean he doesn't have boys?
Ee tata n'abamura atabwati	Ee, doesn't father have boys?
Abamura gesera kenga 'nsembe-eee	Boys who are handsome?
Oraiyaaa, oraiyaa	Oraiyaa, oraiyaa
Chingero bonyangero-ta!	Songs of songs

Nyarokumbo

Boys and girls did not just pick anybody for marriage. Each one was careful to get the right partner. The following song, "Nyarokumbo," indicates how careful girls were when courting. They took time before they accepted the suitor's hand. They subjected boys who came for them to a lot of ridicule and contempt. They made fun of them and teased them. A girl who was visited by a boy will call her friends to come and help to tease him. Let us examine this song, "Nyarokumbo"

Nyarokumbo	**Nyarokumbo**
Nyarokumbo, ee, eyaye, ee	Nyarokumbo, ee, eyaye, ee
Nyarokumbo, ee eyaye, ee	Nyarokumbo, ee, eyaye, ee

Nyarokumbo, ee, eyaye, ee	Nyarokumbo, ee, eyaye, ee
Nyarokumbo 'baiseke ndorere	Nyarokumbo, girls examine him for me
Nyarokumbo 'baiseke ndorere	Nyarokumbo, girls examine him for me
Nyarokumbo, ee, eyaye, ee	Nyarokumbo, ee, eyaye, ee
Nyarokumbo gose n'ekenyonchege	Nyarokumbo, if he is a handsome lad
Nyarokumbo tochi saiga goseka	We can get into the hut to laugh (make love)
Nyarokumbo, ee, eyaye, ee	Nyarokumbo, ee, eyaye, ee
Nyarokumbo onye ne'rititiri	Nyarokumbo, if he is clumsy and old
Nyarokumbo 'motebie anakogenda	Nyarokumbo I tell him to start going away
Nyarokumbo ee, eyaye, ee	Nyarokumbo, ee, eyaye, ee
Nyarokumbo botambe ingokana 'nde	Nyarokumbo because I have always promised
Nyamao tacha minto	Nyarokumbo 'Nyamao' should not visit me
Nyarokumbo, ee, eyaye, ee	Nyarokumbo, ee, eyaye, ee
Nyarokumbo Nyamao obususaire	Nyarokumbo 'Nyamao' who is shivering
Nyarokumbo ekerengesa ngenama	Nyarokumbo with his smoking-pipe across his loin
Nyarokumbo, ee, eyaye, ee	Nyarokumbo, ee, eyaye, ee
Nyarokumbo omosuko embura eratwe	Nyarokumbo during a rainy season
Nyarokumbo ng'ai ndarusie chinko	Nyarokumbo where will I get firewood
Nyarokumbo, ee, eyaye, ee	Nyarokumbo, ee, eyaye, ee
Nyarokumbo ingekerere egesicho	Nyarokumbo to spread his *egesicho* over the fire
Nyarokumbo egesicho kenyakuoma	Nyarokumbo to have his *egesicho* to dry.

In the poem, "Nyarokumbo," the girl tells her friends to examine the man (suitor) who has come to court her. She further implores them that, if they find him handsome, they should let her know so that she would invite him into saiga, a hut, where they (girl and boy) will "laugh" (make romance). But if he is "Nyamao" (a name of a male person, but also symbolic of 'a clumsy, old man who is past the age of marriage), she will tell him to start leaving her home. She, like all other girls, rejected such men. In the song, she complains and ridicules old men (Nyamao) citing that they are difficult to take care of. Why are they difficult? Because they needed a lot of firewood during rainy season, and therefore, she wonders: Where will I get all that firewood from? His egesicho (egesicho was a small piece of cloth the men wore round their hips and covered only the front part of their private parts, leaving the bottoms bare) will need a big fire to dry; where will she get that big fire from? Having asked herself all these questions, she readily dismisses any old man coming to court her.

Because of these difficult situation posed by the girls, boys did not find it easy to court. This led to the engagement of *esigani*, the go-between, who became a bridge between the family of the boy and that one of the girl. The proveb *esigani mboraro nka* (the go-between is a bridge between two families) expresses the function of esigani. The go-between was to help find out about the family of the girl which the boy had identified.

In the absence of *esigani*, things were not easy for the boys who wanted to marry. They laboured for it. The boy had to search, spy, inquire, and gather information about the possible girls he could marry. The girls, on the other hand, did not make it easy for the boys. They hid, concealed information and stayed away from them.

A young man in a group of his friends would lie in wait for a targeted girl on her way to an errand including, to fetch water from the river, or taking goods to the market, or even working on her parents farm. They would then forcefully take her to the young man's hut where she would be kept under very tight security. After one or two days, the young man's parents would visit the home of the girl to report about their 'eng'ondi' sheep which is in the custody of the man's family. ....and things would go on and on...

Apart from the difficulties girls posed to boys in courtship, there was also the issue of dowry. Enough dowry was to be available for a boy to acquire a girl for marriage. The poem, "Nteberie Tata," was sung by a boy while he was far away from home, looking for a girl. In the poem the boy addresses his father. He is pleading with him to do his best to get dowry ready for him to marry. "Nteberie Tata," is set at a girl's home when the boy is pleading with the girl or it is sung by the boy on his way home after he had had a positive response from the girl.

Nteberie Tata	**Tell My Father**
'Nteberie aye tata	Please tell my father
Arabarabe chinyomba chionsi	To search in every house
Tinkwa mogesi ginteneine	So that I don't die a bachelor standing
'Nteberie aye tata	Please tell my father
Arabarabe chinyomba chionsi	To search in every house
Tinkwa mogesi ginteneine	So that I don't die a bachelor standing
Ee, tinkwa mogesi ginteneine,	Ee, I don't die a bachelor standing,
Ee baba	Ee, baba
Tinkwa mogesi ginteneine,	Ee, I don't die a bachelor standing,
Ee, baba	Ee, baba
Tinkwa mogesi ginteneine.	I don't die a bachelor standing.

The poem is a sort of lamentation from a lad who, probably, is past the age of marriage. Having identified a girl to marry, he doesn't want dowry to stand on his way. He tells the father to rescue him from *dying a bachelor standing*. *Dying a bachelor standing* here means that he might be killed while he is looking for a wife. Those days one could be suspected of being a cattle rustler and therefore get killed. His father, therefore, is urgently asked to get dowry to bring this dangerous exercise to an end. *Dying a bachelor standing*, can also be symbolic of 'lust' in the boy. He is assumed to be so lustful (standing) while seducing the girl such that the desire (lust) can overwhelm him and therefore kill him. Since premarital sex was not allowed, his lust, as expressed in the poem, could be understood. To die a bachelor was abominable as one had not left a child to carry his name or lineage to the next generation.

This song, "Monteberie Tata," tells of the significance of dowry. A young man had to secure dowry for his marriage. Sometimes he had to wait untill his sisters got married so as to get dowry for his marriage. Some got past the age of marriage because they could not secure dowry. That is why, around 1950s, Kitutu chief, Zakaria Kirera son of Ooga became popular. This paramount chief came to the limelight because he gave a new decree on bride-price. Why did he give a new decree on brideprice? Mr. Nemwel Mogere Atemba (interview, Kisii, 2017) recalls that in those days pressure to marry was big. It was a must for a boy to marry when he came of age. Because of the pressure that came from the community, boys started stealing cattle from Luoland for purposes of dowry. To discourage this vice, and to help those with over-grown, unmarried young men who could not afford dowry, the chief cut the dowry into half--from twelve cows and one bull to six cows and one bull. In Bonchari, Nyaribari, and Bomachoge clans the dowry remained as before-- twelve cows plus one bull; while in Bobasi Clan the dowry was even higher -- fourteen cows plus one bull. Because dowry in Bogetutu was now lower than before and than elsewhere, boys of age were now able to marry and those already married added more women. Those who were wealthy, in other words had many cows--enjoyed marrying many women. To capture this situation, the conversation would go as follows:

> **Q:** How many cows is he paying for your daughter?
>
> **A:** Six cows and one bull.
>
> **Q:** Okay. I will give you ten cows and one bull.
>
> **A:** Good, you are the one to marry my daughter.

The wealthy had their way, paying less than they used to, but higher than poorer families could afford.

Mr. Nemwel Atemba remembers that men from outside the clan also married from Bogetutu. Some people argue that the chief's decree is the reason why we find Bogetutu women in all parts of Gusii, given the low rates, or affordable dowry.

Names like Nyawaya, Nyakundi, Onsomu and Onsongo were originally of Bogetutu clan, but are now found all over Gusii.

During the decree those with daughters in Kitutu secretly sent them out into other clans like Bonchari, Nyaribari and Machoge where they could fetch a higher bride-price. In the following song the name 'Nyang'wono' means a hero. *Eng'wono*, in Ekegusii, is something amazing or extraordinary. So somebody who is 'Nyang'wono' as in the song below is a hero or one who has done something extraordinary. *Egesicho* is a suit. Instead of saying that the one bull in the dowry was meant for siring with the other six she-cows, the song conceals the puporse and states that the one bull was for *egesicho ki'omogaka* (a suit for the father-in-law).

Kirera ore bw'Ooga	**Kirera, Son of Ooga**
Kirera ore bw'Ooga	Kirera, son of Ooga
Oti Nyagw'ono	Welcome the hero
Akuma isano n'emo	Issued a decree of six
Oti Nyag'wono.	Welcome the hero
N'eyemo y'egesicho	One (bull) for *egesicho* (a suit for the old man)
Oti Nyag'wono	Welcome the hero
N'eyemo y'obokombe	One for the *jembe*
Oti Nyag'wono.	Welcome the hero
Abamura nyuoma bwango	Boys marry in a hurry
Oti Nyag'wono	Welcome the hero
Abamura nyuoma bwango	Boys marry in a hurry
Oti Nyag'wono.	Welcome the hero
Abagaka menta bwango	Old men add more wives
Oti Nyag'wono	Welcome the hero
Abagaka menta bwango	Old men add more wives
Oti Nyag'wono.	Welcome the hero

Mogisangio Akoreke Ekee

Pressure to marry was obvious among young men. The poem, "Mogisangio Akoreke Ekee" (Obino Nyambane, 20th Feb. 2016) is evident that the philosophy of Omogusii was procreation - nothing else. The main value was on cows (brideprice) that brought forth a family.

Mogisangio Akoreke Ekee	**Let the Agemate Weave a Twig-Plate**
Mogisangio akoreke ekee	Let my agemate weave a twig-plate
Ekee nyaboundi	A twig-plate made of straw
Ekee ekio akeimokie	Take the twig-plate
Akegore 'kagena	Trade it with an egg
Akagena ka'ngoko	The egg of a hen
Akagena akwo akaimokie	Take that egg
Akagore mbori	Trade it with a goat
Mbori ere na manwa	A goat with a kid
Ka'bori akwo akaimokie	Take that goat
Akagore ng'ombe	Trade him with a cow
'Ng'ombe euta rioro	A cow that is fat and healthy
'Ng'ombe eyio ayeimokie	Take that cow
Anyegore 'monto	Trade her with a human being (lady)
'Monto aibora abana	The human being to sire children
Abana ebirachuoki	Children that are like fencing trees
Birachuoki mbiagita omochie	Fencing trees protects the homestead.
Omochie egesenyenta!	

Another version of this song was provided and translated by Mzee Nemwel Mogere Atemba and Dr. Matunda Nyanchama (8/03/2019):

Mogisangio Akoreka Ekee	**The Journey towards Plenty**
Mogisangio akoreka ekee – 'kee nyaboundi	Let the agemate weave a twig-plate -- a twig-plate made of straw
Ekee ekio akeimokie, akegore 'kagena – 'kagena ka 'ngoko	Take the twig-plate trade it with an egg -- an egg of a hen
Akagena akwo akaimokie, akagore 'kagoye – 'kagoye ka 'mogondo	Take that egg trade it with a plant rope – a plant rope in the garden
Akagoye akwo akaimokie, akagore 'mbori – 'mbori ere na 'manwa	Take that plant-rope trade it with a goat – a goat with a calf
Embori eyio ayeimokie, ayegore 'ng'ombe – 'ng'ombe euta rioro/ 'ngombe ere na 'mori	Take that goat trade it with a cow - a cow with a calf
Eng'ombe eyio ayeimokie, ayegore 'monto – 'monto aibora bana	Take the cow trade her with a human being – a human being to bear children

Abana ebirachwoki – birachwoki bigita 'mochie	Children that are like fencing trees -- Fencing trees to protect the homestead.
Omochie risangaka -- omochie egesenyenta!	A homestead that is wide -- homestead filled with human beings.

According to Obino Nyambane the above poem carries the omogusii philosophy on hard work, social life and responsibility. A young man was expected to work hard. He could start with something as small as *ekee,* the twig-plate, and proceeded to acquire wealth (prideprice) that enabled him to marry a wife, who in turn gave birth to many children who became *ebirachwoki* (fencing trees) and protected the homestead. *Ebirachwoki* here symbolizes protection that children (youth) were expected to provide to the family, hence the whole community.

Ng'ai Aiga Bwang'ireire

The following song is sung by a boy who had spent a day trying to woo an imaginary girl called Nyarinda. Now that he is coming back home at nightfall, frustrated and tired, he sings the following song:

Nyarinda	**Nyarinda**
Ng'ai aiga bwang'ireire	The night fall has caught up with me
Bwang'ireire Nyakorokomba	At Nyakorokomba
Nyarinda ogera bwang'ireire	Because of Nyarinda
Ng'ai aiga bwang'ireire	The night fall has caught up with me
Bwang'ireire Nyakorokomba	At Nyakorokomba
Nyarinda ogera bwang'ireire	Because of Nyarinda
Ee, bwang'irerire, ee baba	Ee, the night fall, ee, baba
Nyarinda ogera bwang'ireire, ee baba	Nyarinda is the cause, ee, baba
Nyarinda ogera bwang'ireire	Because of Nyarinda
Ng'ai aiga bwang'ireire	The night fall has caught up with me
Bwang'ireire Nyakorokomba	At Nyakorokomba
Nyarinda ogera bwang'ireire	Because of Nyarinda

Ng'ai aiga bwang'ireire The night fall has caught up with me
Bwang'ireire Nyakorokomba At Nyakorokomba
Nyarinda ogera bwang'ireire Because of Nyarinda

Ee, bwang'irerire, ee baba Ee, the night fall, ee, baba
Nyarinda ogera bwang'ireire, ee baba Nyarinda is the cause, ee, baba
Nyarinda ogera bwang'ireire. Because of Nyarinda

Omoiseke Gechemba

Having identified a girl to start courtship with was not the end. The boy was not going to sit on his laurels. He had to consistently work hard to strengthen the relationship. At times, girls made it difficult and any slight slackening by the young man saw his girl wooed by someone else or got convinced by other girls and women in the community to marry someone else. This poem is addressed to an imaginary girl called Gechemba. The boy tells her not to poison the mind of his girl-friend. In the poem the boy addresses Gechemba who was believed to be covetous and a back-biter. The boy is requesting her to spend the night at her parents' home and not with his girlfriend. Since she is jealous and malicious, she is likely to poison the mind of his wife-to-be.

Omoiseke Gechemba **The Girl, Gechemba**

Omoiseke Gechemba The girl, Gechemba
Kore 'mogengi orare seino Since you are a backbiter stay away in your home

Tochia kongengera Sarange So you don't talk ill of me to Sarange

Omoiseke Gechemba The girl, Gechemba
Kore 'mogengi orare seino Since you are a backbiter stay away in your home

Tochia kongengera Sarange So you don't talk ill of me to Sarange

Tochia kongengera Sarange, Ee baba So you don't talk ill of me to Sarange, Ee baba
Tochia kongengera Sarange, Ee baba So you don't talk ill of me to Sarange Ee, baba
Tochia kongengera Sarange. So you don't talk ill of me to Sarange.

Omoiseke Gechemba	The girl, Gechemba
Kore 'mogengi orare seino	Since you are a backbiter stay away in your home
Tochia kongengera Sarange	So you don't talk ill of me to Sarange
Omoiseke Gechemba	The girl, Gechemba
Kore 'mogengi orare seino	Since you are a backbiter stay away in your home
Tochia kongengera Sarange	So you don't talk ill of meto Sarange
Tochia kongengera Sarange,	So you don't talk ill of me to Sarange,
Ee baba	Ee baba
Tochia kongengera Sarange,	So you don't talk ill of me to Sarange
Ee baba	Ee, baba
Tochia kongengera Sarange.	So you don't talk ill of me to Sarange.

Intanyuometi O'Maronga

To find the right girl or man to marry was not an easy task. It involved a lot of effort. The experience was marked with anxiety. A story is told of a boy of a rich man who refused to marry if he was not allowed to marry from a certain home. In the song, "Intanyuometi O'Maronga," the boy is saying that he can only be compelled to marry from Maronga's home where beautiful girls are found. The poet describes Maronga's girls as *abayaye*. *Omoyaye* (singular; plural: *abayaye*) is a word that refers to a girl who is not only beautiful physically, but also neat and intelligent. The soloist also describes the girls as *abasiani* (plural; singular: *omosiani)*, a word that refers to girls who are perfect. Lastly, he describes Maronga's daughters as *chisang'onde,* meaning light-skinned.

In the last stanza of the song the poet changes tune. In a quick rejoinder, he reveals to the audience that he is not serious, but he is only singing, *chingero* (lyrics). This song was sung by a poet with an accompaniment of the *obokano* (the Abagusii eight-string instrument).

Intanyuometi O'Maronga	**If I Don't Marry from Maronga's Family...**
Intanyuometi O'Maronga, omoisia bw'omonda tinkonyuoma !	If I don't marry Maronga's daughter,

Intanyuometi O'Maronga, omoisia bw'omonda tinkonyuoma !	Me, the rich man's son better not marry
Intanyuometi O'Maronga, omoisia bw'omonda tinkonyuoma !	If I don't marry Maronga's daughter,
Intanyuometi O'Maronga, omoisia bw'omonda tinkonyuoma !	Me, the rich man's son better not marry
O'Maronga nao bare bayaye batambe na basiani	At Maronga's one can find the beautiful, the tall, and the perfect
O'Maronga nao bare bayaye batambe na basiani	At Maronga's one can find the beautiful, the tall, and the perfect
O'Maronga nao bare bayaye batambe na basiani	At Maronga's one can find the beautiful, the tall, and the perfect
O'Maronga nao bare bayaye batambe na basiani	At Maronga's one can find the beautiful, the tall, and the perfect
O'Maronga nao bare chisang'onde na basiani	At Maromga's one can find the light-skinned and the perfect
O'Maronga nao bare chisang'onde na basiani	At Maromga's one can find the light-skinned and the perfect
O'Maronga nao bare chisang'onde na basiani	At Maromga's one can find the light-skinned and the perfect
O'Maronga nao bare chisang'onde na basiani	At Maromga's one can find the light-skinned and the perfect
Timokaga 'nabarama ani chingero nabo chiare	Sorry, I am not serious, this is just a lyric
Timokaga 'nabarama ani chingero nabo chiare	Sorry, I am not serious, this is just a lyric
Timokaga 'nabarama ani chingero nabo chiare	Sorry, I am not serious, this is just a lyric
Timokaga 'nabarama ani chingero nabo chiare	Sorry, I am not serious, this is just a lyric

Chapter 5
Oral Poetry during Marriage Ceremonies

An interview with Mzee Nelson King'oina Nyang'era in 2007 reveals the following as the legal procedure regarding proper marriage in the Abagusii community: *Ekerorano* (seeing each other or the meeting of the suitor and the girl's family), *Okomana* (Cattle Culling), *Ogokoba Chiombe* (Escorting Cattle), *Okoira Omoiseke* (Fetching the Girl), *Okobutia* (Honeymoon), *Egechabo* (Return of Wife to her Parents' Home after Okobutia Ocassion), *Egekwano* (Discussion), *Egesabo* (Planning Party), *Egetaorio* (Wrestling of Two Parties), *Echorwa* (The Crowning Ceremony of the Marriage)[1].

During the forth stage of marriage in the Abagusii community, *okoira omoiseke* (taking the bride), the men went to the bride's home to 'capture' her. This activity was an activity characterized by tension and drama. The girl who understood that she was desired and hence worthwhile, was filled with pride. Aware that she was about to be 'captured' and taken away, she hid herself in a home of an aunt, an uncle, a neighbour or a relative who lived far away.

She dodged the suitor and his party who came for her. The men searched for her day and night, in bushes, at her relatives' places, and at any place where they suspected her to be hiding.

The poem, "Nyanduko Mbeche," captures the anxiety that is created during the capture of the bride.

Nyanduko Mbeche	**Nyanduko Mbeche**
Rero ndero	This is the day!
Nyanduko Mbeche	Nyanduko, Mbeche's daughter
Rero ndero	The day has come
Nyanduko Mbeche	Nyanduko, Mbeche's daughter
Riakorigeire korua'gesieri moino	It is staring at you from the doorway

---

1   See also J. S. Akama's *The Gusii of Kenya: Social, Economic, Cultural, Political & Judicial Perspectives.* (Nsemia Inc., 2017)

Oral Poetry in Africa

Konde seito	When at my parent's home
Nigo 'nde Omosongo omogima	I am royalty
'Ngoika bwone	Once married
'Ntebigwe genda saiga	I am told to go into the hut
'Ntebigwe rina borere	Then told to climb up the bed
'Ndine borere	Climb up the bed
Omomura aberebenche	And the man paces around, madly
Toonchore ebinyata	We turn our garments inside-out
Tokore nyantangurera	Then do somersaults

In the first stanza the girl is told that a day has come for her capture. In the second stanza the girl is told what she will expect once the capture is successful. When she is captured and is married, she will be told to go into the hut, and when she does so, she will be told to climb up the bed, and when she climbs up the bed, the lad (husband) will move about madly, and then finally both of them will turn their garments inside-out (remove their clothes), then they will start doing 'gymnastics' (sex). The language employed here is indirect and the poem is powerful in the use of symbolism.

Gesare Kegiteire

The poem, "Gesare Kegiteire" (A Guarded Bean-Plant), talks of one girl, *Gesare,* who is known in Gusiiland to have given boys difficult times in capturing her. Gesare is derived from the name of a certain bean grown in Gusii and whose leaves are part of Abagusii's vegetable milleau.

It is said that Gesare succeeded to dodge the boys for very long and suitor's party almost gave up. However, one day her game came to an end. A boy called Mandere captured her as she was escaping the trap they had laid for her. Both Gesare and Mandere's actions were captured in this song.

Gesare Kegiteire	**A Guarded 'Bean-Plant'**
Gesare kia'Nyaende	Gesare daughter of Nyaende
Gesare kia'Nyaende	Gesare daughter of Nyaende
Gesare kia'Nyaende	Gesare daughter of Nyaende
Bwandire kia'Nyaende	Ooh, of Nyaende

Aye kegiteire	Yeah, guarded
Egesare kegiteire	A guarded bean-plant
Egesare kegiteire	A guarded bean-plant
Bwandire kegiteire	Ooh, guarded
Aya kabagora	Yeah, he broke the fence
Mandere akabagora	Mandere broke the fence
Mandere akabagora	Mandere broke the fence
E bwandire akabagora	Ero, ooh, he broke the fence
Aya aburi ngonko	Aye, they were happy
Agacha amaburi ngonko	Agemates were happy
Agacha amaburi ngonko	Agemates were happy
Bwandire aburi ngonko	Ee, they were happy
Agetureria	He took care of himself
Moumbu agetureria	Moumbi took care of himself
Omoumbu agetureria	Omoumbi took care of himself
Bwandire agetureria	Eh, he took care of himselff
Aye bakagooka	Yeah, they happy
Abakiare bakagoka	Agemates were happy
Abakiare bakagoka	Agemates were happy
E bwandire bakagoka	Ee, agemates were happy

Mong'ererie Ekerori

Now the 'captured' girl is at her husband's home in what is referred to as *Okobutia*. Immediately, or soon after she arrives, the men ensured that the bride was deflowered. According to Nelson Nyang'era, she was deflowered on the thoral bed in the presence of the man's agemates. If she resisted the man, his agemates held her firmly so as to enable the man to deflower her. After assisting in the capturing of the girl and also in ending her virginity, the men were rewarded with a slaughtered hen, cock or a goat. They ate plenty of food. For the woman, deflowering marked the start of the life of being a wife.

According to Nelson Nyang'era, *okobutia* took several weeks. During that period the mother of the bride sent another girl or sister or aunt of the bride with delicious meal to visit the home of the bridegroom. The intention was to find out how they were faring. The visitor was tasked to find out if the marriage had begun successfully. If the marriage had started successfully, they rejoiced and took a message of joy back home. During this time the couple did little work. The two enjoyed sex. The oral poetry during this period was "Mong'ererie ekeroria".

Mong'ererie Ekerori	**Give me a Wind Pipe**
Mong'ererie ekeroria	Give me a wind pipe
'Ng'ende kona kobugia saiga	To play inside my hut
Nario Sarange atachie aande	So that Sarange doesn't desire to go anywhere
Mong'ererie ekerori	Give me a wind pipe
'Ng'ende kona kobugia saiga	To play inside my hut
Nario Sarange atachie aande	So that Sarange doesn't desire to go anywhere
Ee, atachie aande ee baba	Ee, so that she doesn't go out, ee
Nario Sarange atachie aande, ee baba	So that Sarange doesn't go anywhere
Nario Sarange atachie aande	So that Sarange doesn't go anywhere.
Mong'ererie ekeroria	Give me a wind pipe
'Ng'ende kona kobugia saiga	To play inside my hut
Nario Sarange atachie aande	So that Sarange doesn't desire to go anywhere
Mong'ererie ekeroria	Give me a wind pipe
'Ng'ende kona kobugia saiga	To play inside my hut
Nario Sarange atachie aande	So that Sarange doesn't desire to go anywhere
Ee, atachi aande ee baba	Ee, so that she doesn't go out, ee
Nario Sarange atachie aande, ee baba	So that Sarange doesn't go anywhere
Nario Sarange atachie aande	So that Sarange doesn't go anywhere.

In the poem the boy requests for a wind pipe to play while he is with his newly-married wife, Sarange, so that she is not bored and desire to go anywhere. Playing a wind pipe will entertain her and raise her excitement. The pipe symbolizes sex. If the man will play a 'wind pipe', it will keep them busy during the days of *okobutia*.

Christopher Okemwa

Egesike Kiomosogwa

This oral poem is sung during marriage. In the poem women tell the bride the following words of wisdom: *Naumeire egesike kiomosogwa* (I have met a thorn of the tree called *omosogwa*). The women's song is meant to tell the bride that marriage is not a bed of roses; it has its rough side, too. Since she is young she may not understand what marriage is all about. She has got to be prepared for the good and the worst that marriage brings. *Naumeire egesike ki'omosogwa* can also be symbolic of "maleness." A thorn of *omosogwa* tree is known to be the sharpest thorn you can find in the forest. So she is being advised to prepare for sex since she has now met the sharpest thorn, the thorn of *omosogwa* tree.

Egesike Kiomosogwa	**A Thorn of Omosogwa**
Naumeire, 'naumeire	I have met, I have met
Egesike ki'omosogwa	A thorn of omosogwa tree
Naumeire, 'naumeire	I have met, I have met
Egesike ki'omosogwa	A thorn of omosogwa tree
Genda bwango genda bwango	Hurry up, hurry up
Omwanchi one genda bwango	My dear, hurry up
Nkoniga ere, nkonigere kianda	It is going to be tight
Nkoniga ere kianda, koniga ere	It is going to be tight
Baka mambia	Till morning time
Ayerera ayerera	Hurry up, hurry up
Omwanchi one ayerera	My dear, hurry up
Ayerera ayerera	Hurry up, hurry up
Omwanchi one ayerera	My dear, hurry up

Aye Ng'ina Omomura

The song "Aye Ng'ina Omomura," was also sang during marriage ceremonies. The song was collected and translated by Nemwel Mogere Atemba (2018). It goes as follows:

Aye Ng'ina Omomura	**You the Mother of the Bridegroom**
Aye baba ng'ina omumura rende	You the mother of the bridegroom
Ero ombande	There is joy

Soka isiko oiririate rende	Come out and ululate
Ero ombande	There is joy
Kwareteirwe Nyarinda rende	You have been given Nyarinda
Ero ombande	There is joy
N'ere orachie roche rende	She will fetch water from the river
Ero ombande	There is joy
N'ere oratenye chinko rende	She will collect firewood
Ero ombande	There is joy
N'ere orasie orogena rende	She will grind at the grindstone
Ero ombande	There is joy
Nere oraee ng'eni rende	She will look for vegetable
Ero ombande	There is joy
Nere oraigose ngobo rende	She will scrap the hides (clothes)
Ero ombande	There is joy
Aririririiiiiiiiiiiiiii! Aririririiiiiiiiiiiiiii	Aririririiiiiiiiiiiiiii! Aririririiiiiiiiiiiiiii!
Baba ng'ina omoiseke rende	You the mother of the bride
Ero ombande	There is joy
Na'aye kwaigure buya rende	You are the one with the happiness
Ero ombande	There is joy
Kwareteirwe Nyang'era rende	Nyang'era (a cow for prideprice) has been given to you
Ero ombande	There is joy
Nero ereta maguta rende	It will produce butter for you
Ero ombande	There is joy
N'ero ereta kerandi rende	It will give you a gourd (milk)
Ero ombande	There is joy
N'ero ereta kegeni rende	It will bring you.........
Ero ombande	There is joy
Aririririiiiiiiiiiiiiii! Aririririiiiiiiiiiiiiii	Aririririiiiiiiiiiiiiiiii! Aririririiiiiiiiiii!

This song was sung to give advice to the mothers of both the bride and the bridegroom. The song starts by speaking to the mother of the bridegroom. In the song the people tell her to listen to their advice. The song tells her to come out and ululate since it is a happy occasion when her son is getting a wife whose name is Nyarinda. Nyarinda, in the Abagusii community, is a woman who was strong-bodied. Being strong-bodied meant she could fetch water and work hard in the farm. So the mother in the song has a reason why she had to be happy and ululate since the woman which her son had married wouldn't let her down.

In the second stanza, the song addresses the mother of the bride. The song says that she is happy since she has received Nyang'era (bridewealth). Nyang'era in the Abagusii community was a black type of cow that was known to produce plenty of creamy milk that was turned into butter. So the pride's mother had to be happy since the type of cows (bridewealth) she had received were going to give her *amaguta* (milk and butter).

The reader should be aware of the style of singing this song: The soloist will sing the 1st line and all present will respond with the chorus *Ero ombande* (There is joy). The soloist who leads the song will also play the lyre, *obokano* (the eight-string instrument of the Abagusii). He/she will only sing of the benefit the bride and groom's families have received with the marriage. The chorus, *Ero ombande*, acts as an ideophone for the lyre, the 8-string-instrument, and it is sung by the audience and all those present.

More and more stanzas can be added by the soloist as she/he deems fit. The soloist could also 'hand over' the singing to another one and the chain could continue.

Kunora Emboto, Bache Korora.

The following oral poem, *Kunora Emboto, Bache Korora*, collected by Nemwel Mogere Atemba, was sung by men and women when a bride was being dressed ready to go to her new home. The reader should note that this could be a modern version of the song as there were no cars in traditional society. Swahili word 'maridadi' has been obsorbed into, and replaced, Ekegusii word, 'komekameka'.

Kunora Emboto, Bache Korora.	**Shout, Invite Them to Come and See**
Kuunora emboto ee kuunora emboto.	Shout, yes shout
Eee kuunora emboto ee kuunora emboto	Yes, shout, eee shout

Kuunora emboto ee bache korora	Shout, invite them to come and see
Eee bache korora ee bache korora.	Yes, our bride, ee our bride
Bache korora ee omoriakari oito	Shout, invite them to come and see
Eee omoriakari oito ee omoriakari oito	Yes, our bride, yes our bride
Omoriakari oito ee buna achabeire	Our bride, ee she is decorated
Eee buna achabeire ee buna achabeire	Yes she is decorated, yes she is decorated
Buna achabeire ee akomekameka	Our bride, ee she is decorated
Eee akomekameka ee akomekameka	Yes she is decorated, yes she is decorated
Akomekameka ee amaridadi ooka	She is decorated, ee she shines
Eee amaritati ooka ee amaritati ooka	Yes she shines, yes she shines
Rora eee omwana o' Baba,	See yes, my mother's child
Igo are maritati	She is beautiful
Rora eee eanga yaye	See yes, her dress
Igo ere maritati	It is beautiful
Rora eee ekondo yaye	See yes, her scarf/headgear
Igo ere maritati	It is beautiful
Rora eee esuuti yaye	See yes, her suit
Igo ere maritati	It is beautiful
Rora eee ekiore kiaye	See yes, her wedding headgear
Igo kere maritati	It is beautiful
Rora eee egari yaye	See yes, her car
Igo ere maridadi	It is beautiful
Rora eee ONDIEKI o'baba	See yes, ONDIEKI of my mother
Igo are maritati	He is beautiful
Aririririririririiiii	Aririririiiiiiiiiiiiiii
Rora eee MORAA o'mwabo	See his sibling—Moraa

Igo are maritati	She is beautiful
Aririririririririiiii	Aririririiiiiiiiiii
Rora eee ABANA babo	See yes, their children
Igo bare maritati	They are handsome
Aririririririririiiii	Arirririiiiii
Arrririririririiiii	Arirririrriiiiiii

Rero Etaya Yokire

Another song that graced this occasion was 'Rero Etaya Yokire.' It was sung especially by a family that was holding a wedding ceremony for the first time. During this first ever wedding ceremony, everyone is asked to come and witness. The song, in a way, is encouraging girls to be married through wedding ceremonies. This one also is a modern version of the song. The car, as in the previous song, is mentioned and the Swahili word 'maridadi' has been obsorbed to Ekegusii.

Rero Etaya Yokire	**Today a Lamp is Lit**
Aiga seito, intwe intwana gotongia taya	Here at our home, we have never lit a lamp
Aiga seito, intwe intwana gotongia taya	Here at our home, we have never lit a lamp
Aiga seito, intwe intwana gotongia taya	Here at our home, we have never lit a lamp
Rero, eee rero ndero etaya yokire	Today, ee today is the day, the lamp is lit
Rero, eee rero ndero etaya yokire	Today, ee today is the day, the lamp is lit
Rero, eee rero ndero etaya yokire	Today, ee today is the day, the lamp is lit
Aiga seito, intwe intwana korosia e nyangi	Here at our home, we have never had a wedding ceremony
Aiga seito, intwe intwana korosia e nyangi	Here at our home, we have never had a wedding ceremony
Aiga seito, intwe intwana korosia e nyangi	Here at our home, we have never had a wedding ceremony
Rero, eee rero e 'nyangi yachire	Today, eee today, we have a wedding ceremony

Rero, eee rero e 'nyangi yachire	Today, eee today, we have a wedding ceremony
Rero, eee rero e 'nyangi yachire	Today, eee today, we have a wedding ceremony
Aririririririririiii Arrririririririiii	Aririririiiiiiiii, aririiriiiiiiiiiiiiiiiiiii

Refrain:

Rora eee omwana o' baba,	See ee, my mother's child
Igo are maridadi	She is beautiful
Rora eee eanga yaye	See eee, her dress
Igo ere maridadi	It is beauitiful
Rora eee ekondo yaye	See eee, her scarf/headgear
Igo ere maridadi	It is beautiful
Rora eee esuuti yaye	See ee, her suit
Igo ere maridadi	It is beautiful
Rora eee ekiore kiaye	See ee, her wedding headgear
Igo kere maridadi	It is beautiful
Rora eee egari yaye	See ee, her car
Igo ere maridadi	It is beautiful
Rora eee Ondieki o'baba	See ee, ONDIEKI of my mother
Igo are maridadi	He is beautiful
Aririririririririiii	Aririririiiiiiiiiiii
Rora eee Moraa o'mwabo	See his sibling—Moraa
Igo are maridadi	She is beautiful
Aririririririririiii	Aririririiiiiiiiiii
Rora eee Abana babo	See eee, their children
Igo bare maridadi	They are beautiful
Aririririririririiii	Aririririiiiii
Arrririririririiii	Ariririrriiiiiii

Omoiseke Ekenyarokara

While boys married all sorts of girls, the girl most desired by the community was one who was strong and one who could work hard on the farm. In fact boys, in their hunt for wives, could go on spying missions. They could hide somewhere to spy on girls while the latter worked. They would then pick the hard working one among them whom they chose for marriage. A boy who married a lazy woman was unlucky as his parents and the entire community would gossip and make fun of her.

One day, in the history of the Abagusii, a boy married a girl who was lazy, thin and weak, and a poem, "ekenyarokara," was composed for her, which to date is sang to all lazy women.

Omoiseke Ekenyarokara	**A Thin Thing**
Chiombe chia omwana ominto	My sibling's dowry
Nachio chiandentereire	Has brought trouble to my life
'Nkanyuoma ekenyarokara	With it I married a thin thing
Nyamuoroto omogundo	So stinkly lazy
Tachia nachia'mogondo	Can't work on the farm
N'obokima 'nkoriare	Yet the thing eats
Tachi naisana borere	It can't even fill the bed
Ekenyarokara getari na mara 'nda	Thin with no intestines
Chiombe chia omwana ominto	My sibling's dowry
Nachio chiandentereire	Has brought trouble to my life
'Nkanyuoma ekenyarokara	With it I married a thin thing
Nyamuoroto omogundo	So stinkly lazy
Tachia nachia 'mogondo	Can't work on the farm
N'obokima 'nkoriare	Yet the thing eats
Tachi naisana borere	It can't even fill the bed
Ekenyarokara getari na mara 'nda	Thin with no intestines

Weak and likely lazy women were disadvantaged as a woman's value was in her strength to feed her family: her children, her man, his larger family and even the clan. Since there were no jobs in those days, a woman's education or intelligence was not a virtue. Her virtue was measured in the amount of physical strength she embodied or the amount of work she could do on the farm. Woe unto those women who were thin in stature, or weak for that matter. The above poem also says that she is so thin that she can't even fill the bed. It is as if she had no intestines in her stomach. No doubt, well-built, strong women had an advantage, perhaps enjoyed by the men in bed. This is rather contrary with modern (perhaps western) view of a woman's beauty!

Monyenye Moka'Nyatundo

Soon after she started settling in her new home, custom required that the married woman should not look 'cheap'; she had to play a 'reluctant' spouse and unwilling to live in her new home. She had to feign dislike for her marriage, by refusing to eat food served in her new home and even resisted conjugal interaction with her newly-acquired husband. This 'rebellion' or 'defiance' took place for few days, after which she started eating. The following song is about Monyenye Moka Nyatundo. She was the first woman to eat food served at her new home immediately she arrived. She forgot and served herself food and ate, much to the embarrassment of the entire community. The following poem was composed about her.

Monyenye Moka Nyatundo	**Monyenye Wife to Nyatundo**
Ee, Riakeronya,	Monyenye daughter of Keronya
Monyenye Riakeronya	Monyenye daughter of Keronya
Monyenye o Keronya	Daughter of Keronya
Eee, bwandire o' Keronya	Monyenye daughter of Keronya
Aye Bogiakumu	Eeeeh, daughter of Keronya
Agatara Bogiakumu	There at Bogiakumu
Agatara Bogiakumu	She visited Bogiakumu
Eee, bwandire Bogiakumu	She visited Bogiakumu
Aye bondugere	Just cook it for me
Rigembe bondugere	Rigembe cook it
Rigembe bondugere	Rigembe cook it for me
Bwandire bondugere	Eeeh, cook it for me Bogiakumu
Aye okoborundia	Yeah, cook it for me
Agaika okoborundia	She immediately devoured it
Aye bwandire okoborundia	Ooooh, she ate it!

"Monyenye Moka Nyatundo" is a satirical poem. It mocks those women who are too weak to keep the community's cultural beliefs. Monyenye was a woman who was married and, once at her new home, she didn't hesitate to share in the food that was cooked and served. Tradition defined a humble woman as one who didn't readily share in what she was given by her host when she arrived at her new home. She was expected to feign protest and refuse to eat. In those days, a married woman would normally accept food from the neighbours, and not from her new home. Of course sometimes the host would cheat her that the given food was prepared and brought from the neighbouring home, and the girl would then eat it; in that case she was not to blame as she was not aware of the source of the meal. She would eventually start sharing in the family meals, but that happened after days of 'protest/resistance'. Monyenye neither feigned protest nor refused to eat. She started eating once she arrived in her new home, much to the embarrassment, disdain, laughter and amusement of the hosts and the village.

Chapter 6
Poetry for Married Men and Women

These are poems sang for or by married men and women. They either provide advice for living in peace as couples, or advise on behavior and character. You will realize that most of them target women with their messages.

Omosacha N'ere Ritiro

"Mosacha n'ere ritiro," is a poem sang by a married woman. In the poem she tells the other women that they should respect her husband as he is the pillar of their home.

Omosacha N'ere Ritiro	You Badly-Behaved Woman
Omokungu nyagetiara	You woman of no manners
Tonakondamera omosacha	Don't abuse my husband
Nere ritiro rire 'nyomba	He is the pillar in my house
Omokungu nyagetiara	You woman of no manners
Tonakondamera omosacha	Don't abuse my husband
Nere ritiro rire 'nyomba	He is the pillar in my house
Ee rire nyomba, ee baba	The pillar in the house, ee, baba
Nere ritiro rire 'nyomba ee baba	He is the pillar in my house, ee, baba
Nere ritiro rire 'nyomba	He is the pillar in my house
Omokungu nyagetiara	You woman of no manners
Tonakondamera omosacha	Don't abuse my husband
Nere ritiro rire 'nyomba	He is the pillar in my house
Omokungu nyagetiara	You woman of no manners
Tonakondamera omosacha	Don't abuse my husband
Nere ritiro rire 'nyomba	He is the pillar in my house
Ee rire nyomba, ee baba	The pillar in the house, ee, baba
Nere ritiro rire nyomba ee baba	He is the pillar in my house, ee, baba
Nere ritiro rire 'nyomba	He is the hill in my house

A pillar helps the house to stand stable, and without it the house collapses. It is the pillar which holds the house in place. The roof and the thatch are both held in place by the pillar. The poem informs the women that it is men who runs families and make them survive. They are the ones who support and make their families stable. Without a pillar both the roof and the thatch will collapse, just the same way a family without a man will crumble.

Ning'oria?

Like "Omosacha N'ere Ritiro," the following poem entitled *Ning'oria* (Who is that?) is sung by a woman to other women. In the poem, a woman praises her husband.

Ning'oria?	**Who is that?**
Ing'oria okorwa ng'umbu eria?	Who is that coming from the other ridge?
Nigo abwekaine tata	He resembles my father (husband)
Tobaisa komomonya	He shouldn't be the subject of your backbiting
'Ndangererie omwanchi one	Let my love come to me
Omwanchi ondusetie seito	My love who made me a woman
Tobaisa komoaka	Don't hurt him
Tobaisa komomonya	He shouldn't be the subject of your backbiting
Ongoro n'omokunyi	Ongoro is a winner
Ere agakunya isano nemo	He won me with six heifers
Ne echimbori ikomi nemo chioka	And eleven goats
Nachio chiandusia minto	Now I am a woman
Tobaisa komoaka	Don't hurt him
Aaa eeee	Aaa eee
Aaaa eee	Aaaa eee
Tobaisa kong'akera omwanchi one eee	Don't hurt my love
Obe aa eeee	Obe aa eeee

(Orina: 2014:194)

According to Felix Orina Oyioka, the oral poem is sung by a woman to other women. She tells them that her man resembles her own father. "The respect the newly-wed accord her spouse is at the same level as the one she accords her own father, making him such a suitable spouse" (Orina:2004: 98). Orina further states that the woman is protective of her man because of the good things he has done to her. The man is courageous, brave and wealthy and demonstrated that he was able to raise enough for her dowry.

Tinkoaka Moriakari One

The two pervious poems – "Ning'oria" (Orina:2014) and "Omosacha N'ere Ritiro" – indicate love of women for their husbands. The poem, "Tinkoaka Moriakari One," documented by Abai (2015) in his book, *The History and Traditions of the Abagusii People of Kenya: Mwanyagetinge* (2015) indicates love of men for their wives. A man states that he won't batter his wife even if he is compelled to do so.

Tinkoaka Moriakari One	I will Never Beat My Wife
Eee natebigwa ng'a aaka	I was told to beat my wife
'nche tinkoaka moriakari one	I will never beat my wife
Eee natebigwa ng'a aaka	I was told to beat my wife
'nche tinkoaka moriakari one	I will never beat my wife
'nche tinkoaka moriakari one	I will never beat my wife
Kare rogena akona kwemba	When she is grinding and singing
Kare rogena akona kwemba "gotera"	When she is grinding and singing
Kande geta ndora mbosera	And I am seated at *geta* I feel happy
Ndora mbosera	I feel happy
Ndora mbosera	I feel happy
Kande geta ndora mbosera	When seated at *geta*
Ndora mbosera	I feel happy
Ndora mbosera	I feel happy
Kande geta ndora mbosera	When seated at *geta*
Oraiiya-a, oraiiya-a	Oraiiya-a, oraiiya-a
Chingero bonyangero -- taa	Song of songs

Omokungu Sioma Siomia

This song is titled "Omokungu Sioma Siomia" addresses an idle woman who roams in the village visiting other people's homes uninvited and without clear purpose. While in the homes that she visits, she eats food that is given to her. She is mindless and doesn't care whether the food she is given is skimped or was meant for the young children. She also doesn't care which home she visits and any taboo limitations associated with her visits.

This poem condemns her mindless, (implied) lazy nature and lack of self-respect. Women are supposed to be mindful of others, especially the young ones and where there should be moral boundaries. Strong-willed women should not feed before their children eat. They should not accept anyhow what is offered to them by their hosts. Furthermore, they should not roam aimlessly, lest they mess with the community's 'moral code' (*chinsoni*). Women were expected to stay at home where they would be busy with useful household chores.

Omokungu Siomi Siomia	**A Woman Who Roams**
Omokungu sioma siomia	You woman who roams about
Ng'ai okomanya	How do you get to know
Bwarugeirwe	The home where food has been cooked?
Gose mboke	It might be just a morsel
Gose mbwamwana, ee baba	Or be for the baby
Omokungu sioma siomia	You, woman who roams about
Ng'ai okomanya	How do you get to know
Bwarugeirwe	The home where food has been cooked?
Gose mboke	It might be just a morsel
Gose mbwamwana, ee baba	Or be for the baby
Gose mbwamwana,	It might be for the baby
Ee baba	Oh, Oh
Gose mboke	Or small amount
Gose mbwamwana, ee baba	Or be cooked for the baby
Gose mboke	Or small amount
Gose mbwamwana	Or be cooked for the baby

Editor's Note: *the author refers to 'mboke' (a morsel) in this song, there are others that suggest that this is a distortion of the original meaning, where the song should refer to the term was 'mboko' (of the in-laws). In this perspective, the woman in the song would be one who lacks morality, entering any and* all houses/homes (sioma siomia), regardless of whether they are homes of 'in-laws' (boko) or those of people that could be regarded as 'her children' (mbwamwana). 'Sioma Sioma' has an immoral connotation suggesting that such a woman isn't going around just for the sake of it, but perhaps 'sleeping' around recklessly regardless of who she sleeps with, her in-laws, 'her children', etc. Clearly, that would emphasize the issue of 'immorality' as opposed to simple self-respect, thus urging such a woman to respect herself and not be roaming around for immoral purposes

Baba Nyariomana

While "Omokungu Siomia Siomia" condemns a woman who idles around people's homes, "Baba Nyariomana" condemns a woman who is quarrelsome. According to Abai (2015) who has documented this oral poem, the piece warns mothers not to quarrel in the presence of visitors.

Baba Nyariomana	**Quarrelsome Mother**
Eee Nyariomana aye baba	Eee quarrelsome mother
Ninki okonya aye kuomaneire	Why do you quarrel?
Eee Nyariomana aye baba	Eee quarrelsome mother
Ninki okonya aye kuomaneire	Why do you quarrel?
Ninki okonya aye kuomaneire	Why do you quarrel?
Mosuko abageni bare nyomba	Even when we have visitors
Bare nyomba	When we have visitors
Bare nyoma	When we have visistors
Mosuko 'bageni bare nyomba	Even when we have visitors
Bare nyomba	When we have visitors
Bare nyoma	When we have visitors
Mosuko 'bageni bare nyomba	Even when we have visitors
Oraiiya-a, oraiya-a	Oraiiya-a oraiiya-a
Chingero bonyangero -taa	Song of songs

(Abai, 2015)

According to Abai the chant warns mothers not to qurrel in the presence of visitors.

Omokungu Omong'aini

The song "Omokungu Omong'aini" was sung by Pastor Humphrey Moronya (Orina: 2014). It was translated into English by Dr.Felix Orina Oyioka. The song goes as follows:

Omokungu Omong'aini	**A Wise Woman**
Tango omokungu agotacha riiga	I wish for a woman who steps on the firestone
Aroisie endagera	And prepare enough food
Omwana oria	Which the child partakes
Osoka isiko	Before going out into the open
Ekero omogoko oichire gekuba	His chest full of joy
Ochenga nabagisangio baye	To play with age mates
Omogaka obeka ekemigere kiaye	While the man, in his cloth-skin
Oboria keore mang'ana	Sits to interrogate his wisdom and experiences

According to Orina (2014), this oral poem "typically represents the traditional social order with its characteristic hierarchy that placed men at the top followed by women and children" (65). Orina (2014) states:

> The image of a woman working diligently in the kitchen is symbol of submission and order. Her dutifulness made it possible for the man to attend to more important matters of the community (Orina:2014:65).

Orina further states that the "the portrayal of the woman as a passive partner resonates with the realitites of the time which required the married woman to devote her time to the family's welfare and to bringing the children up properly" (65). Orina states that the man's cloth-skin mentioned in the poem is a symbol of status and authority.

Kae Bosibori Ensio yaye

This oral poem "Kae Bosibori Ensio Yaye" is documented in Elder Abai Ochoi's book *The History and Traditions of the Abagusii People of Kenya: Mwanyagetinge* (2015). The poem tells the woman in the neighbourhood to give back Bosibori her grinding stone. The poem states that it is the only one she has for grinding. The poem reads as follows:

Kae Bosibori Ensio yaye	**Give Your Co-Wife Her Grinding Stone**
Eee omokungu oisiko moino	You woman of the other house
Kae Bosibori ensio yaye	Give Bosibori her small grinding stone
Eee omokungu oisiko moino	You woman of the other house
Kae Bosibori ensio yaye	Give Bosibori her small grinding stone
Kae Bosibori ensio yaye	Give Bosibori her grinding stone
Agende kona gosera mwaye	To use in her house
Gosera mwaye	To use in her house
Gosera mwaye	To use in her house
Agende kona gosera mwaye	To go and use in her house
Gosera mwaye	To use in her house
Gosera mwaye	To use in her house
Agende kona gosera mwaye	To go and use in her house
Oraiiya, oraiiya	Oraiiya-a, oraiiya-a
Chingero bonyangero --- taa/ Etago yane mosaiga –taa.	Songs of Songs-- taa /Etago yane mosaiga –taa.

(Abai, 2015)

According to Abai the message of the poem is to encourage co-wives to share household items and to respect one another. But according to Orina (2014) the meaning is deeper than just sharing of household items by co-wives. In the Gusii community men 'entered' a house or houses. In other words men had other women whom they visited and sired children with. This is what we refer to as 'side-chick' or *mpango wa kando* (a sideline arrangement) in the modern times. In Orina's interpretation, the 'grinding stone' symbolizes a man (husband). The woman in the neighbourhhood or co-wife for that matter, is asked "to return Bosibori's grinding stone," in other words, not to stray Bosibori's husband. Orina's version is titled "Mokungu o'Siko Moino"

Mokungu o'Siko Moino	**Woman in the Neighbourhood**
Mokungu o'siko moino	Woman in the neighbourhood
Kae Bosibori	Give Bosibori

Ensio yaye	Her grinding stone
Nero yoka abwate	It is the only one she has
Achie gosera mwaye	She needs to grind flour for her people
Mokungu o'siko moino	Woman in the neighbourhood
Kae Bosibori	Give Bosibori
Ensio yaye	Her grinding stone
Nero yoka abwate	It is the only one she has
Achie gosera mwaye.	She needs to grind flour for her people

(Orina: 2014:197)

Sindigisa Omwana Bw'Omwoyo

This poem is about Sindigisa, daughter of Omwoyo. After her husband died, she started behaving indecently and angaged in immoral activities. Upon examining her conduct, the community was not happy and composed this satirical poem about her. The poem says that all she can do is to 'walk around.' The 'walking around' here refers to 'roaming' and has that negative connotation. It is men who are supposed to 'walk around,' and not women. For women it indicates immorality. The poem also says that she should be provided with a coat (coats were for men) to go and solicit for dowry. Men go out to get dowry and not women.

This appears to be a double standard for the genders in Gusii society. The initial version was:

Tindigiti mok'Omwoyo, Osiririe omogaka moe etaro anya gotara, ee Tindigiti!

Later corrupted (probably by men) into:

Sindigisa omwana bw'Omwoyo, esiri y'omogaka moe etaro anya gotara, ee sindigisa. (The men are justifying their laziness, that it is women that are supposed to work as the men walk around and socialize with others). The socialization may include wife inheritance or even marrying as many wives as can be. No wonder, in the circumcision song; "Oyo oyoo", the boy is encouraged to 'fight' in Kipsigis land, in Masai land and everywhere else. In other words, he can marry as many wives as he can, not to mention, from any corner of this world.

NB: Stanza 2, 3, 4: mention 'Abagaka'(men), proof of the corrupted nature of the song, the men's self defense.

Sindigisa Omwana Bw'Omwoyo	**Sindigisa, Daughter of Omwoyo**
Sindigisa omwana bw'Omwoyo	Ee Sindigisa, daughter of Omwoyo
Osiririe omogaka	She has lost a husband
Moe etaro--ana gotara!	Let her have time—to loiter about
Ee sindigisa	Ee Sindigisa
Sindigisa omwana bw'Omwoyo	Ee Sindigisa, daughter of Omwoyo
Osiririe omogaka	She has lost a husband
Moe etaro--ana gotara!	Let her have time—to loiter about
Ee sindigisa	Ee Sindigisa
Atare Kenyenya e abagaka	Let her loiter at Kenyenya, oh men!
Ee Sindigisa	Ee Sindigisa
Atare Suneka e abagaka	Let her loiter at Suneka, oh men!
Ee Sindigisa	Ee Sindigisa
Atare Keroka e abagaka	Let her loiter at Suneka, oh men!
Ee Sindigisa	Ee Sindigisa
Ee Sindigisa omwana bw'Omwoyo	Ee Sindigisa, daughter of Omwoyo
Osiririe omogaka	She has lost a husband
Moe egoti—achie komana!	Let her have a coat---to go and solicit for dowry
Ee sindigisa	Ee Sindigisa
N'abang'ina ng'ai more?	Women, where are you?
Ee sindigisa	Ee Sindigisa
N'abagaka ng'ai more?	Men, where are you?
Ee sindigisa	Ee Sindigisa
N'abaiseke ng'ai more	Girls, where are you?
Ee sindigisa	Ee Sindigisa
Sindigisa omwana bw'Omuoyo	Ee Sindigisa, daughter of Omwoyo
Osiririe omogaka	She has lost a husband
Moe etaro—ana gotara	Let her have time—to loiter about
Ee sindigisa	Ee Sindigisa

Other than "Sindigisa Omwana Bw'Omoyo" who is sung in this poem, the poem also satirizes women who, when their husbands die, start misbehaving and engaging in immoral acts.

Ng'ererie Obokombe

The oral poem, "Ng'ererie Obokombe" (Orina: 2014), tells of a woman who is a prostitute: According to Orina, this poem symbolically refers to an immoral woman's beauty. He states that it is sex that is symbolized in this poem. A 'hoe' here refers to the 'male reproductive organ and 'sow' refers to 'sex' and 'land' refers to the 'beautiful woman'.

In the song..."Ng'ererie obokombe..." 'Omogondo nyakieni kebariri' is an indicator of the value that was attached to women of brown complexion. At the same time, it refers to the female genatalia (Obscenity).

'Ng'ererie Obokombe	**Give Me a Hoe**
'Ng'ererie obokombe	Give me a hoe
N'ekebago egesera	With a beautiful handle
'Ng'ende koabusera omogondo	So that I may dig
Omogondo nyakieni kebariri	In the land of beautiful red
'Ng'ererie obokombe	Give me a hoe
N'ekebago egesera	With a beautiful handle
'Ng'ende koabusera omogondo	So that I may dig
Omogondo nyakieni kebariri	In the land of beautiful red

(Orina: 2014:102)

Tata n'Omochoberi

Let us now examine the poem "Tata n'Omochoberi," collected by Felix Orina Oyioka (2014). The sentence "he crept on my Mother and brought her home," indicates that the father of the person must have worked hard to get her/his mother as his wife, thus "creeping" upon her. As discussed elsewhere, women in the Gusii traditional context put on a strong 'fight' against being married even when dowry had been paid. The fight was not genuine. They only feigned so that they didn't look 'cheap.'

Tata n'omochoberi	**My Father is a Creeper**
Tata n'omochoberi	My father is a creeper
Agachobera akareta baba	He crept on my mother and brought her home (married her)
N'eng'aya kere 'gekuba	With the big shield before his chest
N'eng'aya kere 'gekuba	With the big shield before his chest
Obe aaa eeeee	Obe aa eeee (interjection for surprise)
Obe aaa eeeee	Obe aa eeee (interjection for surprise)
'Mbura egatwa bokaira	It rained the whole day
Baba tarenge na'gesero	My mother had no skin/hide to lie on
Aaa eeeee	Obe aaa eeee
Aaa eeeee	Obe aaa eeee
Baba tarenge na'gesero	My Mother had no skin/hide to lie on
Obe aa eeee	Obe aaa eeee
Obe aa eeee	Obe aaa eeee
Ng'aki bono kerabe	How will it turn out?
'Bikone mbikone	Miracles are miracles
'Morero oibora 'ibu	Fire begets ashes
'Sasati eibora 'mache	Reeds beget water
Auma aka ng'umbu	Auma (a man's name) get to the other ridge
Kende tikeri 'roche	There is no danger in the valley
Esasati ekona kuoga	The noise you hear comes from reeds
Ing'o bono okoibora aba?	Who bears your kind?
Yaya bamura 'mbare seito	No! We've enough men in our home
Abamura nyakieni 'kebariri	Men of fair complexion
Ebibwato emeng'ento	Men with well-formed thighs
Amaino monwa akengire	Well-formed teeth
Aaa eeee	Obe aaa eee
Aaa eeee	Obe aaa eeee
Abamura n'emeng'ento	
Obe aaa eeeee	

(Orina: 2014:95)

Ruta Omonwa Ochie Nyomba

Mzee Samwel Tamaro Ombasa who sung this *omoino* to me has few kind words for the present generation. The present generation, he states, lacks morals and has simply degenerated beyond traditional expectations. He condemns boys who hug their mothers-in-law, looking at them straight in the eye. It is a shame, he says, and recalls that in the olden days, a young man who is newly-married never faced his mother-in-law. When the two met, the boy shook her hand while looking away from her face. She, too, never looked at her son-in-law straight in the eye. There was that respect.

According to Matunda Nyanchama, this was meant to avert temptations in case the mother-in-law admired the son-in-law or vice versa.

In those olden days, it was expected that when a young man grew up he would get married and sire his own children. When the mother-in-law came to visit such a grown-up man, she was led through a point in the fence and not through *egesieri kiabweri* (the normal gate). This was done so that she could reach *korera yaye* (the boy's mother) first. It was in order that *korera yaye atang'ane komorora* (the boy's mother should see her first).

After his mother-in-law had found her way into the hut and had met with her *korera* (boy's mother), the women who were friends of the man's mother urged him to get into the house so that his mother-in-law could see him. The women told him thus: *genda akorore, nyoko biara aiririate* (get in, let your mother-in-law see you and as a result she will ululate). The following oral poem was sung by the boy:

Ruta Omonwa Ochie Nyomba	**Shout out Till it's Heard in the House**
Ee ruta omonwa ochie'nyomba	Shout out till it's heard in the house
Onteberie omong'ina ng'a baba	Tell it to my mother-in-law
Ee ruta omonwa ochie 'nyomba	Shout out till it's heard in the house
Onteberie omong'ina ng'a baba	Tell it to mother-in-law
Onteberie omong'ina ng'a baba	Tell it to my mother-in-law
Kababa n'oyogosoka 'maiso	She isn't one to look straight in the eye
Ee ruta omonwa ochie 'nyomba	Shout out till it's heard in the house
Onteberie omong'ina ng'a baba	Tell it to my mother-in-law
Ee ruta omonwa ochie 'nyomba	Shout out till it's heard in the house
Onteberie omong'ina ng'a baba	Tell it to my mother-in-law
Onteberie omong'ina ng'a baba	Tell it to my mother-in-law
Ka baba n'oyogosoka 'maiso	She isn't one to look straight in the eye

Gosoka'maiso, 'gosoka 'maiso	Who doesn't look straight in the eye
Ka baba n'oyogosoka 'maiso	She isn't one to look straight in the eye
Ogosoka'maiso	Shout out till it's heard in the house
Ka baba n'oyogosoka 'maiso	Tell it to my mother-in-law
Ogosoka'maiso	Who doesn't look straight in the eye
Ka baba n'oyogosoka 'maiso-ooo	She isn't one to look straight in the eye
Ee ruta omonwa ochie 'nyomba	Tell it to my mother-in-law
Onteberie omong'ina ng'a baba	She isn't one to look straight in the eye
Ee ruta omonwa ochie 'nyomba	Shout out till it's heard in the house
Onteberie omong'ina ng'a baba	Tell it to my mother-in-law
Onteberie omong'ina ng'a baba	Tell it to my mother-in-law
Ka baba n'oyogosoka 'maiso-ooo	She isn't one to look straight in the eye
Oraiyaa, oraiyaa	Oraiyaa, oraiyaa.
Chingero bonyangero-ta!	Song of Songs

Abai has also documented a slightly different version of this oral poem in his book, *The History and Traditions of the Abagusii People of Kenya: Mwanyagetinge* (2015). His version has a different title and reads as follows:

Baba Noyogokumba Riiso

Eee morute omonwa nyomba
Monteberie omong'ina baba
Eee morute omonwa nyomba
Monteberie omong'ina baba

Monteberie omong'ina ng'a baba
Baba noyogokumba riiso

Gokumba riiso
Gokumba riiso
Baba n'oyogokumba riiso

Gokumba riiso
Gokumba riiso

Baba noyogokumba riiso

Oraiya-a, oraiya-a

Chingero bonyangero – taa!

(Abai:2015)

According to Abai this *omoino* states that mother-in-law deserve the greatest respect ever.

Chapter 7
Poetry of Old Age

Abagusii have a proverb that says *'bogotu 'ngesanko,'ngokina kore okuya, 'tangori 'ng'irane 'bwana (obogotu n'egesanko, n'ogokina kore okuya, otangori ing'irane obwana).* This translates to "old age is a crust, or is *egesa na nko,* (a hut and firewood) - always needs firewood for a warm hut; growing up is the good time; I just wish I become young again) (Okemwa: 2012).

This proverb is used by an old person in his/her old age, as a lamentation of his/her helplessness. Old age comes with many problems. In the proverb, *'bogotu bwatenya 'nko na 'nguru, 'ndwari 'mbagori na 'mbogori yatora 'nda, 'nda yanga 'mete a'nchogu nga iroba yasanera* (old age gathers firewood (an old person wants fire all the time) and strength (the fire gives him strength); a given disease breaks out in her/his stomach. She/he is given herbs. The stomach rejects medicine and desires death). This proverb states that at old age the person is vulnerable both to diseases and the environment. At this age the person cannot effectively respond to medicine. The following poem, "Egetiro," passes a similar message as the above proverbs.

Egetiro	**The Hill**
Egetiro kere seito ning'o oragetire?	There is a hill at my home, who can climb it?
Naba 'mogaka ning'o oragetire?	Be it an old man, who can climb it?
Naba 'mong'ina ning'o oragetire?	Be it an old woman, who can climb it?
Naba 'mosacha ning'o oragetire?	Be it a man, who can climb it?
Egetiro kere seito ning'o oragetire	The hill at my home, who can climb it?
Ekero narenge omomura	When I was a young man
Nare gotenga ngokura	I could dance and scream
Bogotu 'ngesanko	Old age is a crust (or, is a hut and firewood)
Ngokina kore okuya	The joy is in growing up.

The poet is an old man. He speaks of the hill found at his home. He asks a series of questions: Who will climb the hill? Can an old man climb it? What of the old woman, will she be able to climb it? Then the questions ceases, as the poet now starts to talk about the past when he/she was young and energetic. He/she says that, when he/she was young he/she could dance and scream. Now that he/she is old he/she cannot dance as he used to. He/she then regrets that old age is a crust (*ngesanko*). Joy is only in being young and growing up. The poem is sung by old men at ceremonies. They sing it to remind themselves of the years gone when they were young and energetic.

Abana Bane

Old age needs support from children, grandchildren and people in the society. Proverbs inform the support that is given to them. The proverb *barande buna 'murwa 'monto narenge o'nyang'au* (let those young boys grow and spread like grass for I would have been eaten by hyenas).

In this proverb an old man blesses young people to thrive. These are young people who assisted him when he was sick and could not walk and was at the risk of being devoured by hyenas. Similarly, in the oral poem, "Abana Bane," an old man praises his/her children for the support they give him/her.

Abana Bane	**My Children**
Abana bane, aiyee, baba aiye	My children, aiyee, baba aiyee
Abana bane Nyambeki na Nyareki	My children Nyambeki and Nyareki
Intabarochi, aiyee, baba aiyee	When I don't see you, aiyee, baba aiyee
Intabarochi nigo 'ngona korangeria	When I don't see you I keep calling
Abana bane aiyee, baba aiyee	My children, aiyee, baba aiyee
Intabarochi nigo 'nkona komagamaga--aiyee	When I don't see you I look around--aiyee
Intabarochi ekero mwachire roche	When you have gone to the river
Nkobasemia aiyee, baba aiyee	I advise you, aiyee, baba aiyee

Mwachire roche gaki mogende ng'ora	When you go to the river walk carefully
Mobuche motire ng'ora	Fetch water and come back home carefully
Emerande n'emekorekanu	Undergrowths can entangle you.
Intabarochi aiyee baba aiye,	When I don't see you yes mother,
Intabarochi enda yane egotera amache aiye!	When I don't see you my stomach is filled with fear

This poem is sung by old women and men. The old man/woman in the song tells his/her children that he gets worried when he doesn't see them around. When they have gone to the river to fetch water he becomes unsettled until they return. He goes ahead to give advice to the children: Walk carefully when you go down to the river because there are many types of undergrowth which can entangle you as you walk back home.

The old people who sung this poem had another meaning underneath this plain one. They meant to advice their children to be careful with extramarital sex. To 'walk carefully' meant 'to abstain oneself from love affairs,' or else one will be entangled (become pregnant for a women or get unwanted children for the man). Sex and love, being taboo subjects, the old people were only able to communicate indirectly, using symbolism.

Chapter 8
Poetry During Death

In this chapter we shall examine several poems that are related to death.

One of the poems we shall look at is "Narire Amabera Ane."

Narire Amabera Ane

This song can be explained as follows: A boy may marry and get a child, but unfortunately that child dies. The death brings much pain and as a result he decides to part with his newly-married wife, blaming her for the death of their child. The father would comfort him, telling him that the dead child is not the only one in his wife's womb. There are many of them and, therefore, he should not divorce her, but plant another seed in her womb. To that advice the boy would sing the following poem:

Narire Amabera Ane	**I have swallowed my bitterness**
Narire amabera ane	I have swallowed my bitterness
Omonyene eng'ombe	I, the owner of dowry
Aboka aichana	Wakes up to sorrow
Tata agantebia beka nende	Father told me to plant another seed
Ee, narire amabera ane	Ee, I have swallowed my bitterness
Omonyene eng'ombe	Me, the one who pays dowry.

Omotakanwa

A woman whose husband dies and leaves her *omotakanwa* (a widow), encounters many challenges: There are fields to be tilled and there are animals to be looked after. Children also demand care from her, which she can't adequately give. The poem, "Omotakanwa," was sang by village people alluding to the widow.

Omotakanwa

Omokungu omotakanwa
Mororere omonanda
Orore buna agotanga
Atange chikomoiriri

Omokungu omotakanwa
Mororere omonanda
Orore buna agotanga
Atange chikomoiriri

Widow

You can tell a widow
At the field palisades
When she grazes herds
She can't control the animals.

You can tell a widow
At the field palisades
When she grazes herds
She can't control the animals.

Chapter 9
Poetry of Inter-clan Skirmishes, Inter-Ethnic Wars, Cattle Rustling and Praise for Animals

Abagusii people had inter-clan skirmishes from time to time. These skirmishes were orchestrated especially by cattle-rustling. In addition they had wars against the hostile and warring communities around them, such as the Maasai and the Kipsigis. In order to protect themselves from other clans and the surrounding communties, the Abagusii devised survival techniques. One technique, according to John S. Akama (2018) was that "the Gusii built homesteads, *omochie*, whose overall physical layout and design took into consideration the safety and protection of the vulnerable members of the family, especially the children, women and the elderly" (ix). He also adds: "...the Gusii had a system in which young men were raised with the conscious aim of protecting their community from enemies" (Akama:2018;ix). During male Circumcision, for instance, the intitates were provided with fighting skills that enabled them to protect their community when they grew up.

The Gusii also had *bisarate* (sing. *gesarate*), which were military camps, established to provide war skills to young people. It is in these camps where young men were trained how to fight against other clans and against their hostile neighbours. Later, as Akama (2018) observes, they used these skills to resist against hostile tribes and the the British colonial rule in Gusiiland.

The oral poems in this chapter capture inter-clan skirmishes and inter-ethnic wars that, majorly, were orchestrated by cattle rustling in Gusii. It also captures oral poetry that praised animals.

Esegi

This poem is sung by Abagusii who live near the borders. At the borders Abagusii sometimes went to war with their neighbours--Kipsigis, the Maasai and the Kuria people. Abagusii rarely went to war against the Luo. This is because the Luos were, at times, supporters of the Abagusii when they were at war. E*segi ya osao osao* (the battle of Mogori) is given as an example of a war in which the Luo supported the Abagusii. You can tell their friendship from the oral poetry sang by the Abagusii during that battle, such as *Sibuor Nyarimo*, songs that originated from Luoland. Most of the Abagusii hero, war and victory songs originated from the Luo since they were the people who fought alongside the Abagusii.

The Luos rarely provoked the Abagusii into war as did the other neighboring tribes. Other tribes, such as the Maasai and the Kalenjinis came to Gusii to conquer them and drive them out. Although the Abagusii were slaves in Luoland at one time, they (the Luos) were humble and only took time to assimilate them.

This song, "Esegi," encourages young men to be brave, strong and always come out to participate in wars against their neighbours. The song advises young men not to be reluctant and let the old men fight for them. The poem is in form of mockery. It ridicules a young man who consults his mother in times of war. Brave young men don't consult their mothers in matters of war, but go straight to the battlefield together with their agemates. It is embarrassing that the young man in this poem has to run to his mother when the war has begun. Such young men are a shame to the community and are marked or noticed or remembered by the community, such that poetry, *chingero bonyangero* (a song of all songs) is composed to satirize them.

Esegi	War
Onye momura kware	If you are a strong boy
Esegi eraa	And here comes a war
Nyoko ogotebia?	Should you consult your mother?
Esegi eraa	And here comes a war

Nyoko ogotebia?	Should you consult your mother?
Otare gotebia	You should've consulted
Mogisangio—oo	Your age-mates-oo
Oraiyaa, Oraiyaa	Oraiyaa, oraiyaa
Chingero bonyangero	A Song of all songs
Seito bonyaseito	Our village, in our village
N'abamura bakwanga	Boys can't come out to fight
N'abamura bakwanga	Boys can't come out to fight
K'abagaka batema emiobo	Old men come out to carry sticks (weapons)
Oraiyaa, Oraiyaa?	Oraiyaa, oraiyaa?
Chingero bonyangero	A song of all songs
Ng'ai abamura bare	Where have the young men gone?
Ng'ai abamura bare	Where have the young men gone?
Chingero bonyangero	A song of all songs

Iyo O Yaye

"Iyo O yaye" is an oral poem collected and sung to me by Dr. Evans Nyamwaka of Kisii University. Nyamwaka recalls that in the late eighties the Majoge people of Gusii planned to steal cattle from Bobasi. The people of Bobasi happened to get wind of the plan and, therefore, planned how to defend themselves as well as kill the Majoge warriors. Nyamwaka narrates that when the Majoge warriors attacked the Ababasi were ready for them. The latter ambushed the Majoge people at a place called Ekebengo, close to Etora. They killed the Majoge warriors and attacked their villages and drove away with cattle. They sung the following song as they came home.

Iyo O Yaye	**Iyo O Yaye**
Iyo o yaye iyo o yaye	Iyo O yaye iyo o yaye
Twabaitire ababisa	We have killed the enemy
Twabaitire Majoge	We have killed Majoge people
O yaye! O yaye	O yaye! O yaye
Ntwe ne'chindo	We are lions
Oyaye!o yaye	O yaye! O yaye
Mbono togocha,	We are now coming
Twachire buya	We have come well.

Iyo o yaye iyo o yaye	Iyo O yaye iyo O yaye
Twabaitire ababisa	We have killed the enemy
Twabaitire Majoge	We have killed Majoge people
O yaye! O yaye	O yaye! O yaye
'Ntwe nechindo	We are lions
Oyaye! O yaye	O yaye! O yaye
Mbono togocha,	We are now coming
Twachire buya.	We have come well.

Motare Goaka Chionsi

"Motare Goaka Chionsi" is *omoino,* a Gusii classic poem, sung to me by Mzee Samwel Ombasa Tamaro. Tamaro narrates that in the old days Maasais and the Kalenjins used to invade Gusii to steal cattle. It is said that one day, Maasai raiders stole all the cows from one village including one cow named *Moikabondo* and its calf. As the invaders drove the cows away, Gusii men followed them. The calf of *Moikabondo* got so tired that it could not walk any more. Since it did not have much value being just a calf, and also the fact that the Maasais don't kill animals, they hid it beside the road and left it there to die.

The Gusii warriors who were chasing after the Maasais came across the calf and carried it back home. For days that followed, the calf was fed, provided with porridge and became a beautiful *ritororo* (heifer). Later, it gave birth to so many calves in that village. The owner was overwhelmed and sung this chant to the Maasai thieves, telling them thus: "If you wanted to leave us poor you could also have taken the calf of Moikabondo." He sung the following chant:

Motare goaka chionsi	**You Could Have Taken All**
Ee motare goaka chionsi	Ee, you could have taken all
Moake n'emori a'Moikabondo	Including the calf of Moikabondo
Motare goaka chionsi	Ee, you could have taken all
Moake n'emori a'Moikabondo	Including the calf of Moikabondo
Moake n'emori a'Mokaibondo	Take the calf of Moikabondo
Eakanie amagoro amakaru	Walk it on weak legs

E amakaru, e amakaru	E weak, e weak
Eakanie amagoro amakaru	Wobbling, weak legs
E amakaru	Weak
Eakanie amagoro amakaru	Wobbling, weak legs
E amakaru	Weak
Eakanie amagoro amakaru	Wobbling, weak legs
Motare goaka chionsi	Ee, you could have taken all
Moake n'emori a'Moikabondo	Including the calf of Moikabondo
Motare goaka chionsi	Ee, you could have taken all
Moake n'emori a'Moikabondo	Including the calf of Moikabondo
Moake n'emori a'Mokaibondo	Take the calf of Moikabondo
Eakanie amagoro amakaru	Walk it on weak legs
Oraiyaa, oraiyaa	Oraiyaa, oraiyaa
Chingero bonyangero-ta!	Song of songs.

Omachoge Nochirera

"Omachoge Nochirera" is *omoino*, a Gusii classic poem, sung to me by Mzee Samwel Ombasa Tamaro. He states that Bomachoge and Bogirango are two neighbouring clans in Gusii. In the olden days, the two engaged in cattle-theft from each other. The following chant is sung by Abagirango to Abamachoge men. They are telling them that their cattle are well-guarded by their warriors and, therefore, they cannot steal them.

Omachoge nochirera	**Machoge, Even if You Desire**
Ee Omachoge nochirera	Yes, Machoge, even if you desire them!
Ee tokonyora ng'ombe a'Girango	Yes you cannot get the cows from Bogirango
Ee Omachoge nochirera	Yes, Machoge, even if you desire them
Tokonyora ng'ombe a'Girango	Yes you cannot get the cows from Bogirango

Ee tokonyora ng'ombe a'Girango	Yes, you cannot get the cows from Bogirango
Chiabogeire gochia emenyinkwa	They are securely protected in the shrubs
Gochia emenyinkwa, gochia emenyinkwa	In the shrubs, in the shrubs
Chiabogeire gochia emenyinkwa	They are securely protected in the shrubs
Gochia emenyinkwa	In the shrubs
Chiabogeire gochia emenyinkwa	They are securely protected in the shrubs
Gochia emenyinkwa	In the shrubs
Chiabogeire gochia emenyinkwa	They are securely protected in the shrubs
Ee Omachoge nochirera	Yes, Machoge, even if you desire
Tokonyora ng'ombe a'Girango	Yes you cannot get the cows from Bogirango
Ee Omachoge nochirera	Yes, Machoge, even if you desire
Tokonyora ng'ombe a'Girango	Yes you cannot get the cows from Bogirango
Tokonyora ng'ombe a'Girango	Yes, you cannot get the cows of Bogirango
Chiabogeire gochia emenyinkwa-aaa	They are securely protected in the shrubs
Oraiyaa, oraiyaa,	Oraiyaa, Oraiyaa
Chingero bonyangero-ta!	Songs of songs-ta!

Endabu Ekare o'Mogendi

Once upon a time in Bogirango, at Tabaka, a man called Mogendi had a white bull called *Endabu*. The bull was strong and won every fight it had with other bulls. Because of its strength, Abamachoge wanted to take it away. Abagirango teased Abamachoge by telling them that their (Abagirango) bull is spotless white and Abamachoge might grime it with their dirty hands. So when the fight between them began, Abagirango would dare Abamachoge by telling them, thus "Touch it, or Take it away, and you will see!"

Endabu Ekare o'Mogendi	**The White One at Mogendi's**
E, endabu ekare o'Mogendi	The spotless white one at Mogendi's
Endabu ekare o'Mogendi-i-i-i	The spotless white one at Mogendi's--ii
E, endabu ekare o'Mogendi	E, the spotless white one at Mogendi's
Endabu ekare o'Mogendi	E the spotless white one at Mogendi's
Otayeakire 'mbiro--aaaaa	You might grime it with soot--aaa
E, endabu ekare o'Mogendi	The spotless white one at Mogendi's
Endabu ekare o'Mogendi-i-i	The spotless white one at Mogendi's--ii
Ee, endabu ekare o'Mogendi	E, the spotless white one at Mogendi's
Endabu ekare o'Mogendi	E the spotless white one at Mogendi's
Otayeakire 'mbiro--aaaaa	You might grime it with soot--aaa
Endabu ekare o'Mogendi--aaaaa	The spotless white one at Mogendi's--aaaa
Otayeakire 'mbiro--aaaa	You might grime it with soot--aaaa

Enyakoria ya Moseti

A certain man at Tabaka, in South Mugirango, had a bull called *Nyakoria* which was also strong like *Endabu* discussed above. Abagirango used to pride themselves and teased Abamachoge, thus "Nyakoria ya Moseti only eats our limesalt in Bogirango and not someone else's. Furthermore, no one can take it away." They were being contemptuous, insulting and arrogant during war time. They told Abamachoge that they (Abamachoge) could not afford to feed it. "It can't eat your limesalt," they mocked them, "other than our own limesalt." They dared them to take it away from Bogirango people: "Come and take it, here it is!" they mocked.

Enyakoria ya Moseti	**Moseti's Bull**
Ee Enyakoria ya Moseti	Ee Moseti's bull
Nyakoria ya Moseti-i-i-i	Nyakoria of Moseti – i-i-i
Ee Enyakoria ya Moseti	Ee the bull of Moseti
Nyakoria ya Moseti	Nyakoria of Moseti
Etakoria 'bara yonde-- aaaa	He who eats no one's limesalt

Ee Enyakoria ya Moseti	Ee the bull of Moseti
Nyakoria ya Moseti-i-i-i	Nyakoria of Moseti – i-i-i
Enyakoria ya Moseti	Ee the bull of Moseti
Nyakoria ya Moseti	Nyakoria of Moseti
Etakoria 'bara yonde-- aaa	He who eats no one's limesalt
Enyakoria ya Moseti--aaaa	The bull of Moseti –aaaa
Etakoria 'bara yonde--aaaaa	He who eats no one's limesalt ---aaaa
Enyakoria ya Moseti--a aaa	The bull of Moseti –aaaa
Etakoria 'bara yonde--aaaaa	He who eats no one's limesalt ---aaaa

Kemwama Eeri Kianera Nda

Other than the previous two poems – "Endabu Ekare Omogendi" and "Enyakoria ya Moseti" – that pour praises upon a bull, this oral poem, "Kemwama Eeri Kianera Nda," documented by (Abai :2015) in his book, also praises a certain bull due to his prowess in fighting other bulls.

Kemwama Eeri Kianera Nda	**Our Black Strong Bull**
Eee ngosikina ere roche	Eee Looking for a bull to fight with
Kemwama ngosikina ere roche	Our black strong bull is looking for a bull to fight with
Eee ngosikina ere roche	Eee Looking for a bull to fight with
Kemwama ngosikina ere roche	Our black strong bull looking for a bull to fight with
Kemwama ngosikina ere roche	Our black strong bull looking for a bull to fight with
Kemwama ne'eri kianera nda	He has a spontaneous voice
Kianera nda	A spontaneous voice
Kianera nda	A spontaneous voice
Kemwama ne'eri kianera nda	Our black strong bull has a spontaneous voice
Kianera nda	A spontaneous voice
Kianera nda	A spontaneous voice
Kemwama ne'eri kianera nda	Our black strong bull has a spontaneous voice

Oraiiya-a, oraiya-a   Oraiiya-a, oraiiya-a
Chingero bonyangero –taa   Song of songs -taa

Maura Ere

Like the last three previous oral poems - "Endabu Ekare Omogendi", "Enyakoria ya Moseti" and "Kemwama Eeri Kianera Nda" —this poem, "Maura Ere," sung by Timothy Nyarera Ongubo praises a bull that every family wants. The bull is in the centre of families who want their daughters to be married by the owner of the bull. The song says that the cow is scrambled upon by all people because it is a good cow.

Maura Ere	**Eee, He is scrambled upon by All**
Ee maura ere	He is scrambled upon by all
Eeri yaito maura ere	Our bull is scrambled upon by all
Ee maura ere	He is scrambled upon by all
Eeri yaito maura ere	Our bull is scrambled upon by all
Ekieni kiaye	Its beauty is scrambled upon
Maura kere	It is scrambled upon
Orogendo rwaye	Its gait is scrambled upon
Maura rore	It is scrambled upon
Rigori riaye	Its price is scrambled upon
Maura rire	It is scrambled upon
Okorema kwaye	Its ploughing is scrambled upon
Maura kore	It is scrambled upon
Ee maura ere	He is scrambled upon by all
Eeri yaito maura ere	Our bull is scrambled upon by all
Ee Maura ere	He is scrambled upon by all
Eeri yaito maura ere	Our bull is scrambled upon by all

N'abamura 'Ngebura

This chant was composed and sung for young men in Gusii. Young men are supposed to be strong and able to defeat enemies during war. Even if some die in war, more are born. Young men are equated to *'mbisiringi,* a type of tree in Gusiiland that sheds leaves and grows some more. Young men, like *ebisiringi,* die in war but are replaced by those that are born.

N'abamura 'Ngebura	**Young Men Win Wars**
Ee n'abamura 'ngebura	Ee young men win wars
N'abamura 'ngebura--aaaa	Young men win wars
Ee n'abamura 'ngebura	Ee young men win wars
Na 'bamura 'ngebura	Young men win wars
Babura bande oboe--aaaa	Take grazing fields from others
Ee n'abamura 'ngebura	Ee young men win wars
Na 'bamura 'ngebura	Young men win wars
N'abamura 'ngebura--aaaa	Young men win wars – aaa
Ee n'abamura 'ngebura--aaaa	Ee young men win wars –aaa
Na 'babura bande oboe--aaaa	Take away grazing fields from others –aaa
Ee n'abamura 'ngebura--aaa	Ee young men win wars –aaa
Ee 'babura bande oboe--aaaa	Ee take away grazing fields from others -- aaa
Ee n'abamura 'ngebura--aaaa	Ee young men win wars –aaa
Ee 'babura bande oboe--aaaa	Ee take away grazing fields from others -- aaa
Ee abamura 'mbisiringi	Ee young men win wars –aaa
Ee abamura 'mbisiringi--iiii	Ee take away grazing fields from others -- aaa
Abamura 'mbisiringi	Ee young men are ebisiringi trees
Bamura'mbisiringi	They die, others grow
Bagokwa bagobona—aaaa	
Ee abamura 'mbisiringi	Ee young men are ebisiringi trees
Bamura 'mbisiringi-i-i	They die, others grow

Ee abamura 'mbisiringi	Ee young men are ebisiringi trees
Bagokwa bagobona—aaaa	They die, others grow
Ee abamura 'mbisiringi--aaaa	Ee young men are ebisiringi trees—aaa
Ee bagokwa bagobona--aaaa	Ee they die, others grow –aaa
Ee bagokwa bagobona--aaa	Ee they die, others grow --aaa

Nyamwambaro Orotandi

The following *omoino* was sung to me by Peter Nyamache Getenga.

Nyamache recounts that Nyaribari is comprised of a number of sub-clans including Abatondo, Abakimotwe, Abataranda, Abaguche, Abamwaboto, Abanyakoni, Abamobea, Abanyamoyio, Abanyamasicho, and Abamwamoriang'o. In Nyaribari the group called Onyangore Orobara (Kamba Nane) is comprised of few of the above that is Abataranda, Abamwaboto, Abanyakoni, Abamobea, Abanyamoyio, Abanyamasicho and Abamwamoriang'o.

In the old days, Abanyangore could find themselves in skirmishes with *Abamanyi,* the Maasai. Many of the warriors died in the process. Twenty six (26) of the warriors who fought but survived are still remembered to date. They are Oruru Getenga, Otenyo Getenga, Anyona Nyakiore, Nyakebake Obare, Gwoka Getenga, Nuguti Getenga, Kerochi Mogeni, Mogeni Mogeni, Oboki Mogeni, Ong'uti Mogeni, Mauti Osiemo, Nyabuga Mochoge, Omwata Mochoge, Nyagekong'o Mochoge, Nyagwondo Obare, Mageto Mangoyia, Isoka Kirotwa, Miyogo Getenga, Onchuru Obare, Kimikimi Ogendi, Mang'iti Getieseremi, Nyakiongora Nyakondo, Oreti Matara, and Sakagwa Matara.

In 1887 the 26 surviving warriors went to war against Ababasi (people from Bobasi) at a place called *Ebisarate bia'Kagwori* (ebisarate of Kagwori), near the land where Nyanko Secondary school is currently build. Indigiti Bagwasi and Bosire Getenga (aka Kego) were the fiercest of the Abanyangore warriors. The two led a contigent of the 26 warriors to fight Ababasi (people from bobasi).

Among the Ababasi people were two fierce warriors called Oreko (Omosansa) from Bosansa area and Omageri from Masige area. These two were strong-bodied men. The two opponents, Indigiti Bagwasi and Bosire Getenga had *chibarate* (singular *ebarate*). These were big spears like those the Biblical Pharoh carried with the help of other people. In addition, Bosire Getenga had *omwambaro* (*engobo y'esegi*), amour of war.

During the fight, Indigiti Bagwasi speared Omageri who ran with the spear in his back till he reached his home—Masige. He bled to death. On the other hand Bosire Getenga fought Oreko Omosansa and defeated him, by throwing him down.

After this defeat Oreko O'Mosansa made friendship with his opponent, Bosire Getenga and could come over to visit him from time to time. Men and women sung the following *omoino*, (classical poem), "Nyamwambaro Orotandi."

Nyamwambaro Orotandi	**Nyamwambaro Orotandi.**
Oreko oria Omosansa	Oreko from Bosansa
Iya iya iya iya-aaa	Iya iya iya iya-aaa
Oreko oria Omosansa	Oreko from Bosansa
Iya iya iya iya-aaa	Iya iya iya iya-aaa
Ning'o ore komochika	Who invited him?
Iya iya iya iya-aaa	Iya iya iya iya-aaa
Ning'o ore komochika	Who now invites him?
Iya iya iya iya-aaa	Iya iya iya iya-aaa
'Nkego ore komochika	It is Kego who invites him
Iya iya iya iya-aaa	Iya iya iya iya-aaa
Nyamwambaro orotandi	It is Kego who invites him
Iya iya iya iya-aaa	Iya iya iya iya-aaa
Nyamwambaro orotandi	Nyamwambaro orotandi (a praise name for Kego)
Iya iya iya iya-aaa	Iya iya iya iya-aaa

Onyangore amang'eng'a	Nyamwambaro orotandi
Iya iya iya iya-aaa	Iya iya iya iya-aaa
Onyangore amang'eng'a	The one who strayed dowry meant for Mosiori's daughter
Iya iya iya iya-aaa	
	Iya iya iya iya-aaa
Akang'enga echia Mosiori	The one who strayed dowry meant for Mosiori's daughter
Iya iya iya iya-aaa	Iya iya iya iya-aaa
Akang'enga echia Mosiori	When beer was already fermenting in pots
Iya iya iya iya-aaa	Iya iya iya iya-aaa
Ka 'maroro are enyongo	When beer was already fermenting in pots
Iya iya iya iya-aaa	Iya iya iya iya-aaa
Ka 'maroro are enyongo	When beer was already fermenting in pots
Iya iya iya iya-aaa	Iya iya iya iya-aaa

In the above oral poem, Bosire Getenga, the fierciest warrior of the Abanyangore (Abanyaribari), is praised by being referred to as Kego. He is also praised by being called "Nyamwambaro orotandi" (because he carried *omwambaro* (*engobo y'esegi*), amour of war. But he is also refered to as "the one who strayed dowry meant for Mosiori"

This latter point reminds us why Abanyaribari are referred to as "Abanyaribari Amang'eng'a." Mzee Nemwel Mogere Atemba tells me this story: Once upon a time there was a boy from Bomachoge clan who had identified a girl, a daughter of Mosiori, probably from Bobasi. The boy's agemates and his people set out with dowry to go and get the girl. On their way, they had to pass through Nyaribari clan. As they drove the cows, they met with a family who admired their cows and duped them into marrying their daughter. The party never proceeded to the home of Mosiori, whose daughter was intended to be married. True as the Abagusii proverb states *gia'koboko ke'monwa aare* (that which is in the hand is far from the mouth); there is no guarantee that what is in the hand will get to be eaten (or ever land in the mouth).

Apart from the above instance that Mzee Nemwel Atemba narrates, there are many tales of cases in Nyaribari clan where families conspire to stray a man into marrying from a family he never intended. Mzee Atemba gives the following as a typical case.

A group of men driving cows (meant for dowry) to a girl's home would be met by a family. The family could either be having many unmarried, eligible girls, or would just happen to admire the cow(s) the men are driving. The family would, tactifully, stray the men by welcoming them to their home, pretending to be hospitable and kind. The old man in that home, during their conversation, would then deceive the visitors into believing that the home they were heading to for purposes of courtship had issues or was not good. He would speak in parables, innuendoes and illusions about the home of the bride-to-be. For instance, he would say: *ebisieri morasieke bokong'u, mosiekere ebiige* (you will be made to lock your doors tightly at night, lock them using *ebiige*). This is an indirect way of saying that the family to which the men are taking brideprice do practise witchcraft. But before the visitors could digest the indirect reference by the old man, the latter would shout to his daughters: *tema emori, Kemunto ng'ayi baachia?* (Kemuto where have you gone? I want you to drive away the visitors' cows).

The visitors, who would be left to ponder the matter on their own, would consider themselves lucky to have come across this new family otherwise they could have fallen into trouble had they been left to proceed to the home of the intended bride. The old man would swiftly come around again to add something in parables: *'nchera teri gotebia 'monto* (the road does not tell someone what is ahead). In other words these young men who were on their way to their bride's home could not possibly know what would befall them in the end. Indirectly, the old man is implying that he had rescued them from entering into a relationship 'destined' to be bad.

Believing this to be true and a genuine help from this family, the suitors would give up going to their planned destination. Instead, they would decide to go back home. However, before leaving, the old man would come around to bid them goodbye, and while doing so, he would call his daughter and say: "Kemunto, *Koba abageni*" (Kemunto, escort the visitors). The daughter would escort the visitors. On the way she would sweet-talk them, show love and understanding and the men would be excited and fall in love. Kemunto would end up not coming back, but would now get married to one of the boys.

That is why there is a saying in Gusii that *Nyangore Amang'eng'a akang'eng'a echia Mosiori kagichigocha nka* (the people from Nyaribari, are called *Nyangore Amang'eng'a*, who strayed the cows that were a bride price for Mosiori's daughter).

Onkware Okare o Mogendi

Onkware was a fast runner in Bogirango clan. During war he could chase the enemy and get hold of him. When caught, he could run away from the enemy without being captured. He was of light-skinned complexion.

Onkware Okare o Mogendi	**Onkware Son of Mogendi**
Ee Onkware n'onsegereria	Ee Onkware is a dove
Onkware n'onsegereria	Onkware is a dove
Ee Onkware n'onsegereria	Ee Onkware is a dove
Onkware n'onsegereria	Onkware is a dove
Onkware okare O'Mogendi--aaaa	Onkware son of Mogendi –aaaa
Ee Onkware n'onsegereria	Ee Onkware is a dove
Onkware n'onsegereria--aaaa	Onkware is a dove
Ee Onkware n'onsegereria	Ee Onkware is a dove
Onkware n'onsegereria	Onkware is a dove
Onkware okare O'Mogendi--aaaa	Onkware son of Mogendi –aaaa
Onkware okare o'Mogendi---aaaa	Onkware son of Mogendi –aaaa
Onkware magoro mango--aaaa	Onkware with fast legs –aaaa
Ee amagoro mabariri--aaaa	Ee light-skinned legs –aaaa
Ee amagoro mabariri--aaaa	Ee light-skinned legs --aaaa
Onkware n'onsegereria--aaaa	Onkware is a dove --aaaa

Orangi Aka Ng'umbu

There were two sub-clans in South Mugirango clan in Gusii: Borangi and Boisanga. Abarangi (the people from Borangi), although small in number, used to defeat Abaisanga (the people from Boisanga) during war. One old man from Boisanga clan told another old man from Borangi clan, thus: "let us have peace between us". The old man from Borangi agreed to create peace and hence went and passed the information to his people. After receiving the information, the Abarangi men refused to accept the proposed peace. The old man warned them, thus: "you mean you have defied my plea for peace and prefer to live in perpetual antagonism towards our neighbours, the Abaisanga? It is alright, go ahead and continue fighting with them. But remember that Abaisanga are more in number and if we continue to fight, no matter how skillful we are, our men will be finished while Abaisanga will have some of their men remaining to fight on!" He sung the following *omoino* (classical poem) as a warning to the young men:

Orangi Aka Ng'umbu	**People from Bogirangi**
Ee Orangi aka ng'umbu	Yes Abarangi cross the river
Ogonche chinguba chinakuoma	Make shields and let them dry
Ee, Orangi aka ng'umbu	Yes Abarangi cross the river
Ogonche chinguba chinakuoma	Make shields and let them dry
Ogonche chinguba chinakuoma	Make shields and let them dry
Oisanga rogoro n'enga mache	Abaisanga are many like the sea
Ee n'enga 'mache, e n'enga 'mache	Yes they are like a sea, like a sea
Oisanga rogoro n'enga 'mache	Abaisanga are many like a sea
E n'enga 'mache	Yes, like a sea
Oisanga rogoro n'enga 'mache	Abaisanga are many like a sea
E n'enga 'mache	Yes, like a sea
Oisanga rogoro n'enga 'mache-eee	Abaisanga are many like a sea

Ee, Orangi aka ng'umbu	Yes, Abarangi cross the river
Ogonche chinguba chinakuoma	Prepare shields and let them dry
Ee Orangi aka ng'umbu	Yes Abarangi cross the river
Ogonche chinguba chinakuoma	Prepare shields and let them dry
Ogonche chinguba china kuoma	Prepare shields and let them dry
Oisanga rogoro n'enga 'mache-eee	Abaisanga are many like the sea
Oraiyaa, oraiyaa	Oraiyaa, oraiyaa,
Etago yane 'mosaiga.	My etago, friend

Once the old man sung this chant, the Abarangi men decided to obey him and sought peace. But they told him, thus: "but tell them to respect us!" With this the two sub-clans came together and lived in peace. To this date Abarangi and Abaisanga respect each other and have never fought.

Mogekobe Okwerera

In Machoge clan of Gusii, we have a story of Mogekobe and his only son, Ndege. When Ndege grew up, he started fighting or wrestling with boys who were bigger than him, and defeating them. Being the only child, his mother became worried in case he got killed by bigger boys. When she talked about her worry to her husband, the latter dismissed her. However, the old man later became equally worried about their only son. But he wondered where he was going to hide the son so that he is not killed. His son now had enemies everywhere --the Abanchari, Ababasi, and Abagirango – who could be hiding behind *emiobo* (type of trees in Gusii). The phrase *gesongo keroro kere omwobo* (the bitter poison among the *emiobo* trees) refers to the many enemies the boy had made. *Gesongo* was poison applied to the tip of the arrows used for fighting. The following chant is sung by the old man, as he wondered where he would hide his only son from his enemies.

Mogekobe Okwerera	**Mogekobe Crying**
Ee Mogekobe okwerera	Ee Mogekobe crying
E kai 'ngochia kobisa Ndege	E where will I hide Ndege?

Ee Mogekobe okwerera	Ee Mogekobe crying
E kai 'ngochia kobisa Ndege	E where will I hide Ndege?
E kai 'ngochia kobisa Ndege	E, where will I hide Ndege?
Gesongo keroro kere omwobo	A bitter poison is among the *emiobo* trees
Kai 'ngochia kobisa Ndege	E, where will I hide Ndege?
Egesongo keroro kere omwobo	A bitter poison is among the *emiobo* trees
Kere omwobo, kere omwobo	Among *emiobo* trees, among *emiobo* trees
Egesongo keroro kere omwobo	A bitter poison is among the *emiobo* trees
Kere omwobo	Among *emiobo* trees
Egesongo keroro kere omwobo	A bitter poison is among the *emiobo* trees
Kere omwobo	Among *emiobo* trees
Egesongo keroro kere omwobo	A bitter poison is among the *emiobo* trees
Ee Mogekobe okwerera	Ee Mogekobe crying
Kai ngochia kobisa Ndege	E where will I hide Ndege?
Ee Mogekobe okwerera	Ee Mogekobe crying
Kai ngochia kobisa Ndege	E where will I hide Ndege?
Kai ngochia kobisa Ndege	E, where will I hide Ndege?
Egesongo keroro kere omwobo	A bitter poison is among the *emiobo* trees
Oraiyaa, oraiyaa	Oraiyaa, Oraiyaa
Etago yane 'mosaiga	My red-ochred friend.

Morembe Tori Kwangwa

A tale is told regarding the Abagusii and the Luo. In those old days when Abagusii fought with the Luo, it is said that the person Abagusii feared most was Abiti, a tall huge, fearsome Luo. Abiti had a friend called Radenda who was equally massive in stature.

In the Abagusii community there was also a young boy called Sagwe, a cousin of Onkeo. Sagwe was small, but fierce and strong. One day, Sagwe wanted to go and beat the two Luo men—Abiti and Radenda. People advised him that it could be good for him to grow up first and be a little more stronger. Sagwe defied the advice. He started off with his cousin, Onkeo. They carried *chinguba* (shields made from cow-hide). When they reached river Mosache at Riosiri, at a place called Ria'Tong'i, as luck would have it, they came face to face with Abiti and Radenda who had come to fight the people of Bosinange in Gusii. Abiti told Radenda: "We have found "food" (an enemy to fight); our walk is not for nothing. I thought our walk could bear no fruits. We are lucky it can now bear fruits."

Sagwe who was fiercer than Onkeo told Abiti thus: "You have *ching'aya* (bigger shields meant for the whole body, also made from cow-hide) and we only have *chinguba* (normal size shields), furthermore you are bigger than us. If you fight us you will definitely defeat us because we have small shields and we are younger than you." It was also not allowed for someone to fight another if the other did not call for the fight.

"Whom are you telling," Abiti roared. "If you are not ready, you are going to die."

Sagwe quickly whispered to his cousin, Onkeo: "Pair with Radende, he seems to be the softer of the two, and less skilled."Onkeo obeyed and moved closer to Radende. "Let me take on this hyena," he said as he took on Abiti, the fierce, the bigger and the more skilled fighter.

"Abiti if you have no sympathy, get ready, do what you want to do. We are men like you," Sagwe dared. "*Abamura 'mbanga bande!*"(Men are like any other!), he hissed.

They fought. Abiti thought it was going to be a walk-over but found Sagwe difficult to beat. Suddenly Sagwe heard his friend, Onkeo, crying: "Sagwe, Radende is killing me!" Sagwe responded by jumping up and spearing Abiti. While Abiti fell down, he jumped up again and landed on Radende. Soon the fight was over and the two fierce Luo warriors lay defeated!

The following chant was sung by the Abagusii. The chant tells Abiti, who was the fiercer of the two Luo men, to accept peace that Sagwe had asked him to embrace. The word *Nyamaiya* used in the song refers to a scene of fighting.

Morembe Tori Kwangwa	**Peace Never Refuses**
Ee 'morembe tori kwangwa	Ee, peace never refuses
Abiti 'morembe tori kwangwa	Abiti, peace never refuses
Ee 'morembe tori kwangwa	Ee, peace never refuses
Abiti 'morembe tori kwangwa	Abiti, peace never refuses
Abiti 'morembe tori kwangwa	Abiti peace never refuses
E toira abamura Nyamaiya	E, don't take boys to Nyamaiya (the scene of fighting)
Tori kwangwa, tori kwangwa	Never refuses, never refuses
Abiti 'morembe tori kwangwa	Abiti, peace never refuses
Tori kwangwa	Never refuses
Abiti 'morembe tori kwangwa	Abiti, peace never refuses
Tori kwangwa	Never refuses
Abiti 'morembe tori kwangwa	Abiti, peace never refuses
Ee 'morembe tori kwangwa	Ee, peace never refuses
Abiti 'morembe tori kwangwa	Abiti, peace never refuses
Ee 'morembe tori kwangwa	Ee, peace never refuses
Abiti 'morembe tori kwangwa	Abiti, peace never refuses
Abiti 'morembe tori kwangwa	Abiti peace never refuses
Toira abamura Nyamaiya	E, don't take boys to Nyamaiya (a scene of fighting)
Oraiyaa, oraiyaa	Oraiyaa, oraiyaa
Chingero bonyangero-ta!	Song of songs-ta!

Omonyangeteti Bwama

This *omoino* (classical poem) is about Abanchari clan of Gusii. In this chant Abanchari who felt despised by Abagirango clan, refer to themselves as Omonyageteti. So Omonchari (a person belonging to Abanchari clan) advises another one from the same clan to give birth to so many children so that their clan can have many men and therefore will become strong against Abagirango in war. Both *Omonyangeteti* and *Omosangora* (shrubs) plants symbolize Abanchari people. The two plants are known to bear many seeds, thereby symbolizing prolific multiplication and bearing of many offspring. In the *omoino* 'chinsonga' means the tip of the spears. Therefore, the line *Tororie chinsonga Bogirango* means "we point our spears towards Bogirango" (In other words "we fight the Abagirango").

Omonyangeteti Bwama	**Omonyangeteti Grows**
Omonyangeteti bwama	Omonyangeteti sires
Otebia omosangora 'ng'a twame	Tells omosangora to also sire
Ee omonyangeteti bwama	Omonyangeteti sires
Otebia omosangora 'ng'a twame	Tells omosangora to also sire
Otebia omosangora 'ng'a twame	Tells omosangora to also sire
Tororie chinsonga Bogirango	We point spears towards Bogirango
E Bogirango, e Bogirango	E Bogirango, E Bogirango
Tororie chinsonga Bogirango	We point spears towards Bogirango
E Bogirango	E Bogirango
Tororie chinsonga Bogirango	We point spears towards Bogirango
Bogirango	E Bogirango
Tororie chinsonga Bogirango-ooo	We point spears towards Bogirango
Omonyageteti bwama	Omonyangeteti sires
Otebia omosangora 'ng'a twame	Tells omosangora to also sire
Ee omonyangeteti bwama	Omonyangeteti sires
Otebia omosangora 'ng'a twame	Tells omosangora to also sire
Otebia omosangora 'ng'a twame	Tells omosangora to also sire
Tororie chinsonga Bogirango-o-o-o	We point spears towards Bogirango
Oraiyaa, oraiyaa	Oraiyaa oraiyaa
Chingero bonyangero-ta!	Song of songs-ta!

Kai aa Chiakiriria

Tales are told of the old times when Abanchari and Abagirango used to fight at their border, near Esae River at the place called Kerina. From the Abanchari clan there was a man called Itibigu who had killed a lot of people from Bogirango. His mother used to ululate and praise him. She took pride in the son. One day one man from Bogirango volunteered to take a fight with him. People gathered to see another win for the son of Itibigu. The unexpected thing happened. Within a short time the man from Bogirango, who many thought was going to be crashed, speared the son of itibigu. The mother, who used to think that there was no any other mother who had given birth to a strong boy, was so disappinted. Abagirango sang the following omoino.

Kai aa Chiakiriria	**Where Do Our Cows Graze?**
Ee kai aa chiakiriria?	Ee, where do our cows graze?
Echiaito n'Esae chiakiriria	Ours graze by river Esae
Ee kai aa chiakiriria?	Ee, where do our cows graze?
Echiaito n'Esae chiakiriria	Ours graze by river Esae
Echiaito n'Esae chiakiriria	Ours graze by river Esae
Moka'Itibigu agakwa ribetu	Itibigu's wife died of envy (disappointment)
Agakwa ribetu, agakwa ribetu	Died of envy, died of envy
Moka'Itibigu agakwa ribetu	Itibigu's wife died of envy (Disappointment)
Agakwa ribetu, agakwa ribetu	Died of envy, died of envy
Moka'Itibigu agakwa ribetu	Itibigu's wife died of envy (Disappointment)
Agakwa ribetu, agakwa ribetu	Died of envy, died of envy
Moka'Itibigu agakwa ribetu	Itibigu's wife died of envy (Disappointment)
Ee kai aa chiakiriria?	Ee, where do our cows graze?
Echiaito n'Esae chiakiriria	Ours graze by river Esae
Ee kai aa chiakiriria?	Ee, where do our cows graze?
Echiaito n'Esae chiakiriria	Ours graze by river Esae

Echiaito n'Esae chiakiriria Ours graze by river Esae
Moka'Itibigu agakwa ribetu Itibigu's wife died of envy (disappointment)

Oraiyaa, Oraiyaa Oraiyaa, Oraiyaa
Etago yane 'mosaiga My etago, friend.

Enyang'au Y'Egetonto

In the Abagusii community cattle-theft was rampant. A thief would hide in the bamboo forest and waylay cattle that came to the river to drink water and steal some. A chant was composed for such a thief who would hide in the bamboos and escape with cattle. Such a thief is being referred to by this *omoino* as *enyang'au y'egetonto* (a hyena of the bamboo forest). The *omoino* states that he makes fire to warm himself as he waits for the cattle. In those old days fire was made by rubbing two dry sticks together, thus the line *esegese omorero* (rub sticks to make fire) in the poem.

Enyang'au Y'Egetonto **The bamboo forest hyena**
Ee 'nyang'au y'egetonto Ee the bamboo forest hyena?
Esegese omorero enagwota Makes fire to warm himself

Ee 'nyang'au y'egetonto Ee the bamboo forest hyena
Esegese omorero enagwota Makes fire to warm himself

Esegese omorero enagwota Makes fire to warm himself
Eganyere chimori chia'Kimaiga To waylay Kimaiga's cattle

E chia'Kimaiga, e chia'Kimaiga E Kimaiga's, e kimaiga's
Eganyere chimori chia'Kimaiga To waylay Kimaiga's cattle

E chia'Kimaiga E Kimaiga's
Eganyere chimori chia'Kimaiga To waylay Kimaiga's cattle

E chia'Kimaiga E Kimaiga's
Eganyere chimori chia'Kimaiga--aaaa To waylay Kimaiga's cattle-aaaa

Ee 'nyang'au y'egetonto Ee the bamboo forest hyena
Esegese omorero enagwota Makes fire to warm himself

Ee'nyang'au y'egetonto	Ee the bamboo forest hyena
Esegese omorero enagwota	Makes fire to warm himself
Esegese omorero enagwota	Ee the bamboo forest hyena
Eganyere chimori chia'Kimaiga--aaaa	Makes fire to warm himself
Oraiyaa, Oraiyaa	Makes fire to warm himself
Etago yane 'mosaiga	To waylay Kimaiga's cattle—aaaa

Timokaga Mba'manyi

In the olden days Abagusii and their neighbouring tribe—the Maasai—used to go for war at the border market of Ibencho. One day the Abagusii designed a strategy to kill as many Maasais as possible. Half of them clad themselves in *shukas*--the Maasai attire--while the others dressed in the usual clothes of the Abagusii. When the Maasais came to the border, the Abagusii group of warriors dressed like them went round and surrounded them. The Maasais, upon seeing them, thought they were part of their group. They were surrounded by the two groups of Abagusii warriors. The following chant captures what the group of Abagusii warriors who were dressed like Maasai warriors were telling the other group dressed in usual clothes of the Abagusii: "Don't think we are Maasais; we are *okione* camouflaged so that we can fight from behind the hill of Ibencho." 'Okione' is part of the Abamachoge clan of Gusii. This tactic of fighting the Maasai was developed in the area because of interaction with the Maasai and didn't happen elsewhere in Gusii.

Timokaga Mba'manyi	**Don't Mistaken Us for Maasai Warriors**
Ee timokaga 'mba'manyi--iii	Don't mistaken us for Maasai warriors
Abaisia n'okione yeonchoire	We are okione camouflaged
Ee timokaga 'mba'manyi--iii	Don't mistaken us for Maasai warriors
Abaisia n'okione yeonchoire	We are okione camouflaged
Abaisia n'okione yeonchoire	We are okione camouflaged
Erwane ribencho korwa moino	So as to ambush the enemy behind Ibencho hill

Abaisia n'okione yeonchoire	We are okione camouflaged
Erwane ribencho korwa moino	So as to ambush the enemy behind Ibencho hill
E korwa moino, e korwa moino	Behind Ibencho hill, behind Ibencho hill
Erwane ribencho korwa moino	So as to ambush the enemy behind Ibancho hill
E korwa moino	Behind Ibencho hill
Erwane ribencho korwa moino	So as to ambush behind Ibencho hill
E korwa moino	Behind Ibencho hill
Erwane ribencho korwa moino-ooo	So as to ambush the enemy behind Ibencho hill
Ee timokaga mba'manyi--iii	Don't mistaken us for Maasai warriors
Abaisia n'okione yeonchoire	We are okione camouflaged
Ee timokaga 'mba'manyi--iii	Don't mistaken us for Maasai warriors
Abaisia n'okione yeonchoire	We are okione camouflaged
Abaisia n'okione yeonchoire	We aer okione camouflaged
Erwane ribencho korwa moino--ooo	So as to ambush the enemy behind Ibencho hill
Oraiyaa, oraiyaa,	Oraiyaa, Oraiyaa
Chingero bonyangero--ta!	Song of Songs---ta!

Rinyanda ria Mongei

People of Bogirango used to fight amongst themselves with fighting sticks. A family which didn't belong to the clan of Rinyanda ria'Mongei used to be mocked that they cannot fight Rinyanda ria'Mongei, a big pot-bellied man. No one reached close to him when they fought with sticks. They had to group themselves into a formidable force so as to fight him, but even so they didn't move him an inch. Omooga was his really name but was nicknamed *Rinyanda*. Rinyanda (big-stomached) was a praise name. Mongei was his father.

Rinyanda ria Mongei	**Pot-Bellied Man Son of Mongei**
Ee rinyanda ria Mongei	Ee pot-bellied man son of Mongei
Rinyanda ria Monge-i-i-i	Pot-bellied man son of Mongei
Ee rinyanda ria Mongei	Ee, pot-bellied man son of Mongei
Rinyanda ria Mongei	Pot-bellied man son of Mongei
Nyanda ekorara riyo--aaaa	Big stomach lying on a hide
Ee rinyanda ria Mongei	Ee pot-bellied man son of Mongei
Rinyanda ria Mongei--iii	The huge man of Mongei
Ee rinyanda ria Mongei	Ee, pot-bellied man son of Mongei
Rinyanda ria Mongei	Pot-bellied man son of Mongei
'Nyanda ekorara riyo--aaaa	Big stomach lying on a hide
Ee rinyanda ria Mongei--aaaa	Ee pot-bellied man son of Mongei--aaaa
Enyanda ekorara riyo--aaaaa	Big stomach lying on a hide--aaaa
Ee Rinyanda ria'Mongei--aaaa	Ee pot-bellied man son of Mongei--aaaa
Enyanda ekorara riyo--aaaaa	Big stomach lying on a hide--aaaa

Kwamboka Ng'ina Amwata

A long time ago Abagirango and Abamachoge used to fight. Abagirango also used to fight the Luo, their neighbours. In the Abagirango clan there was a woman who used to go near the border of the enemies and pretend to collect firewood. She was safe since women were never killed in skirmishes. Each time she saw the enemy coming, she hid behind bushes and stole away quickly to alert her people. Because of her bravery, she became popular and the following *omoino* was composed for her by men.

Kwamboka Ng'ina Amwata	**Kwamboka, Amwata's Mother**
Ee Kwamboka ng'ina Amwata	Eee, Kwamboka, Amwata's mother
Kwamboka ng'ina Amwata--aaaaa	Eee, Kwamboka, Amwata's mother
Ee Kwamboka ng'ina Amwata	Eee, Kwamboka, Amwata's mother
Kwamboka ng'ina Amwata	Eee, Kwamboka, Amwata's mother
Gachie osiomeri moino--aaaa	Go and spy in the yonder--aaaaaa
Ee Kwamboka ng'ina Amwata	Eee, Kwamboka, Amwata's mother
Kwamboka ng'ina Amwata--aaaa	Eee, Kwamboka, Amwata's mother

Ee Kwamboka ng'ina Amwata	Eee, kwamboka, Amwata's mother
Kwamboka ng'ina Amwata	Eee, kwamboka, Amwata's mother
Gachie osiomeri moino--aaaaa	Go and spy in the yonder--aaaaaa
Ee gachie osiomeri moino--aaa	Ee go and spy in the yonder--aaaa
Orore gose bagocha--aaaa	See if the enemy's coming--aaaa
Orore gose bagocha--aaaa	See if the enemy's coming--aaaa
Okurere emerimana	Alert those unaware
Okurere emerimana--aaaa	Alert those unaware
Okurere emerimana	Alert those unaware
Okurere emerimana	Alert those unaware
Emerimana emeuko--aaaa	Those unaware and blind
Ee okurere emerimana	Ee alert those unaware
Okurere emerimana--aaaa	Alert those unaware--aaaa
Ee okurere emerimana	Ee alert those unaware
Okurere emerimana	Ee alert those unaware
Emerimana emeuko--aaaa	Those unaware and bind
Emerimana emeuko--aaaa	Those unaware and blind--aaaa
Emeuko etakorora--aaaaa	The blind who cannot see--aaa

Omonto Okonywa Amarwa Aya

In the previous poem we saw Kwamboka Ng'ina Amwata, a woman who helped Abagusii men in spying the enemies. In this poem we meet Kemunto, a woman who applied magic to trap the enemies.

It is said that in the olden days Maasais used to come at night and kill the villagers in Gusii and drive away their cows. Kemunto from Bogirango clan had *ebiranya* (sort of magic). When she applied the magic, it made the Maasai warriors to be easily trapped. It is said that, at one time, they came straight into the middle of the village where Abagusii were able to kill all of them. Kemunto became popular in the community. Unlike other women who were prohibited from drinking liquor in the public, she became an exception and was allowed to intermingle with men and drink with them in the public. In the following chant the men are saying: "Whoever is drinking liquor let him share it with Kemunto, mother of Ong'ono."

Omonto Okonywa Amarwa Aya	**Whoever Drinks This Liquor**
Ee, omonto okonywa amarwa aya	Whoever drinks this liquor
Asibie Kemunto ng'ina Ong'ono	Share it with Kemunto, mother of Ong'ono
Ee, omonto okonywa amarwa aya	Whoever drinks this liquor
Asibie Kemunto ng'ina Ong'ono	Share it with Kemunto, mother of Ong'ono
Asibie Kemunto ng'ina Ong'ono	Share with Kemunto, mother of Ong'ono
Kan'ere 'monto 'mayianda agoita	She is the one overwhelmed by sympathy
'Mayianda agoita, 'mayianda 'goita	Overwhelmed by sympathy, overwhelmed by sympathy
Kan'ere 'monto 'mayianda agoita	She is the one overwhelmed by sympathy
'Mayianda agoita	Overwhelmed by sympathy
Kan'ere 'monto 'mayianda agoita	She is the one overwhelmed by sympathy
'Mayianda agoita	Overwhelmed by sympathy
Ka n'ere 'monto 'mayianda agoita	She is the one overwhelmed by sympathy
Ee, omonto okonywa amarwa aya	Whoever drinks this liquor
Asibie Kemunto ng'ina Ong'ono	Share it with Kemunto, mother of Ong'ono
Ee, omonto okonywa amarwa aya	Whoever drinks this liquor
Asibie Kemunto ng'ina Ong'ono-oooo	Share it with Kemunto, mother of Ong'ono
Asibie Kemunto ng'ina Ong'ono	Share it with Kemunto, mother of Ong'ono
Kan'ere 'monto 'mayianda agoita	She is the one overwhelmed by sympathy

Oraiyaa, Oraiyaa,	Oraiyaa, oraiyaa
Etago yane'mosaiga	Songs of songs-ta!

Ninki Otabori Atama?

This chant is about the people of Botabori sub-clan who used to live around Tabaka. Mogendi, who was Omorangi the leader at Tabaka, was despised by this people, Abatabori. Omorangi was joined by their uncles—Abasinange -- to chase away Abatabori.

Ninki Otabori Atama?	**Why have Abatabori Cowardly Run away?**
Ee ninki Otabori atama?	Ee, why have Abatabori cowardly run away?
Ninki Otabori atama—aaaa?	Ee, why have Abatabori cowardly ranaway?--aaaa
Ee ninki Otabori atama?	Ee, why have Abatabori cowardly run away?
Ninki Otabori atama?	Ee, why have Abatabori cowardly run away?
Omorangi omosinini--aaaa	Because of the small number of Abarangi people--aaaa
Ee ninki Otabori atama?	Ee, why have Abatabori cowardly run away?
Ninki Otabori atama—aaa?	Ee, why have Abatabori run away?--aaaa
Ee ninki Otabori atama?	Ee, why have Abatabori cowardly run away?
Ninki Otabori atama?	Ee, why have Abatabori cowardly run away?
Omorangi omosinini—aaaa	Because of the small number of Abarangi people--aaaa
Ee ninki Otabori atama—aaaa?	Ee, why have Abatabori cowardly run away?
Omorangi omosinini--aaaa	Ee, why have Abatabori cowardly run away?
Omorangi onchera igoro--aaa	Because of the small number of Abarangi people--aaaa
E Omorangi n'egesuka--aaa	Abarangi is a strong weed
Ee n'ere Otabori atama--aaa	He is the cause of Abatabori cowardly running away
Agatama korwa Tabaka--aaaa	They cowardly went away from Tabaka--aaaa
Agatama korwa Tabaka--aaaa	They cowardly went away from Tabaka--aaaa

Ee Sanyera Abanto

This oral poem is documented and translated by John S. Akama in his book, *The Gusii of Kenya: Social, Economic, Cultural, Political and Judicial Perspective* (2017). The author says that the song was sung in 1896 by the Abagusii people "on their way home after vanguishing the enemy" (30) during the osaosao battle. In this battle the author notes:

> ...a whole generation of Kipsigis warriors was wiped out. The pitched battle was so intense that the water of the adjacent mogori and Charachani rivers turned red due to human blood oozing out of the bodies of the butchered Kipsigis warriors whose bodies were thrown in the river (30)

The oral poem states that "Don't think Mogori battle is the same as Ngarora" (31). Ngarora is another battle that the Abagusii fought earlier against the Maasais that was led by their leader Ongarora (thus, Ngarora battle). In this battle the leader, Ongarora, was felled and the Abagusii retreated. In this regard the song states that Mogori battle is favourable to Abagusii as compared to Ngarora in which they were repulsed by their enemy.

Ee Sanyera Abanto	**Unite All the Gusii Warriors**
Ee sanyera abanto	Unite All the Gusii Warriors
Ee sanyera abanto	Unite All the Gusii Warriors
Ee sanyera abanto	Unite All the Gusii Warriors
Ee sanyera	Yes, unite
Ee sanyera	Yes, unite
Ee sanyera	Yes, unite
Tokaga Mogori nero Ngarora	Don't think Mogori battle is the same as Ngarora
Ee sanyera	Yes, unite
Ee sanyera abanto	Unite All the Gusii Warriors
Ee sanyera abanto	Unite All the Gusii Warriors
Ee sanyera abanto	Unite All the Gusii Warriors

Ee sanyera	Yes, unite
Ee sanyera	Yes, unite
Ee sanyera	Yes, unite

(Akama:2017:30)

Chiachire

This oral poem is documented and translated by John S. Akama in his book, *the Gusii of Kenya: Social, Economic, Cultural, Political and Judicial Perspective* (2017), in which he discusses the epic war that emerged between the Abagusii and the Kipsigis at Kabianga in the late 19th Century. In this war, the author states that "the Gusii people were ruthlessly attacked and uprooted by the marauding Kipsigis warriors targeting the priced Gusii cattle" (179). It was this massive loss of cattle and the hopeless situation that the Abagusi found themselves in that this song was sung.

Chiachire	**The Cows have been Taken Away**
Mbweri are	The catte rustler is inside the cattle shed
Mbweri are eee	The cattke rustler is inside the cattle shed
Mbweri omorumbwa Arap Chuma	The cattle rustler Arap Chuma from Rumbwa
Chiachire eee	The cows have been taken away
Chiachire chiombe chiomogesi	The cows belong to a senior bachelor
Kura mono eee	Meant for his dowry have been stolen
Kura mono Moraa kura mono	Make the distress call moraa to awaken the warriors
Kura mono Moraa kura mono	Make the distress call moraa to awaken the warriors
Beng beng titi beng beng waya	Beng beng titi beng beng waya

"Beng beng titi beng beng waya" *(Rhythmical sound imitating Gusii traditional musical instrument called obokano (lyre)*

(Akama:2017:180)

Natebibwe Ng'a Tanga

A story is told of a man who lived near River Gucha in Gusii. He used to graze his cows near the river and the cows drank water from the river. One day, he noticed *omogumo* tree that grew near the river and had its branches that straggled all over and some immersed in the water. He thought about what those branches were doing in the water. To him they seemed as if they were trying to block water from flowing by. But he could see that, albeit the effort by the boughs of the tree, the water swiftly flowed by. He sympathized with the tree for its failure to block the water. One day, he decided to give support to the tree. He climbed down to the river and, standing beside the boughs, he blocked the water with his massive hands. Much to his chagrin, he realized that the water still flowed with ease past his fingers. He regretted and said: "I will not manage to block the water from its line of flow, let the boughs and the branches do it. Not me." So he sung the following chant.

Natebibwe Ng'a Tanga	**I have been asked to Block**
Ee natebibwe ng'a tanga	Ee, I have been asked to block
Amache a'Gucha inche tingotanga	I cannot block the water of the Gucha (River)
Ee natebibwe ng'a tanga	Ee, I have been asked to block
Amache a'Gucha inche tingotanga	I cannot block the water of the Gucha (River)
Amache a'Gucha inche tingotanga	I cannot block the water of the Gucha (River)
Orotu mote ronagotanga	Let the Mogumo-tree block
Ronagotanga, ronagotanga	Let it block, let it block
Orotu mote ronagotanga	Let the mogumo-tree block
Ronagotanga	Ee, I have been asked to block
Orotu mote ronagotanga	Let the mogumo-tree block
Ronagotanga	Let it block, let it block
Orotu mote ronagotanga	Let the mogumo-tree block
Ee natebibwe ng'a tanga	Ee, I have been asked to block

Amache a'Gucha inche tingotanga	I cannot block the water of the Gucha (River)
Ee natebibwe ng'a tanga	I cannot block the water of the Gucha (River)
Amache a'Gucha inche tingotanga	Let the Mogumo-tree block
Amache a'Gucha inche tingotanga	Let it block, let it block
Orotu mote ronagotanga-aaaa	Let the mogumo-tree block
Oraiyaa, oraiyaa	Oraiyaa, oraiyaa
Chingero bonyangero-ta!	Songs of songs-ta!

Timbwati Ng'ombe Egochena Mache

This chant was sung by a man who had only young cows and one big one called *Nyasamo*. When the animals were taken to the river, the young ones walked ahead, leaving *Nyasamo* behind. By the time *Nyasamo* was at the river, the young ones had drank their share and in the process made the water dirty. The owner sung this chant to persuade *mame* (his maternal uncle) to give him mature cows like *Nyasamo*. Although *mame* means maternal uncle, in this context the word does not directly refer to the latter, but is used as an expression. In other words, the poet is thinking aloud and to him, *mame* refers to nobody in particular.

Timbwati Ng'ombe Egochena Mache	**I have No Cow to Clean the Water**
Ee, timbwati ng'ombe mame	Ee, I have no cow Uncle
Timbwati ng'ombe egochena 'mache	I have no cow to clean the water
Ee, timbwati ng'ombe mame	Ee, I have no cow Uncle
Timbwati ng'ombe egochena 'mache	I have no cow to clean the water
Timbwati ng'ombe egochena 'mache	I have no cow to clean the water
Nyasamo n'etintira egocha enywa	Nyasamo drinks dirty water
Ee gocha enywa, ee egocha enywa	Ee drinks, ee drinks
Nyasamo n'etintira egocha enywa	Nyasamo drinks dirty water

Egocha enywa	Ee drinks
Nyasamo n'etintira egocha enywa	Nyasamo drinks dirty water
E egocha enywa	Ee drinks
Nyasamo n'etintira egocha enywa	Nyasamo drinks dirty water
Ee, timbwati ng'ombe mame	Ee, I have no cow Uncle
Timbwati ng'ombe egochena 'mache	I have no cow to clean the water
Ee, timbwati ng'ombe mame	Ee, I have no cow Uncle
Timbwati ng'ombe egochena 'mache	I have no cow to clean the water
Timbwati ng'ombe egochena 'mache	I have no cow to clean the water
Nyasamo n'etintira egocha enywa-aaaa	Nyasamo drinks dirty water
Oraiyaa, oraiyaa	Oraiyaa, oraiyaa
Chingero bonyangero-ta!	Song of songs-ta!

According to Jane Obuchi, here, the poet is lamenting on the disrepute that he experiences from his fellow villagers just because he does not have an energetic herd. The water is deliberately guarded by the villagers who know very well that by the time his cow gets to the river, all the other cows will have drunk and made dirty the water in the river. Being a non entity in his village, he has no audacity to complain about the water being dirty. He is thankful, though, that his cow, Nyasamo, is able to bear up with the state of affairs that of drinking dirty water.

Onchari Nkorere're

This chant is about Abanchari clan of the Abagusii community. Legend has it that a long time ago, as they migrated to present-day location, they came from forests around Lake Victoria. At one time they looked around and saw Manga hill. They admired the hill and started wishing the hill could be a part of their land. They wished they could live on the hill and grow as a community, spread and expand. The following chant is about their wish to acquire Manga hill.

Onchari Nkorere're	**Bonchari People Cry that**
Ee Onchari 'nkorere're--ee	We the Bonchari people cry that
Otangori e'Manga ebe yane	Manga hill could be mine
Ee Onchari 'nkorere're -- ee	We the Bonchari people cry that
Otangori e'Manga ebe yane	Manga hill could be mine
Otangori e'Manga ebe yane	I wish Manga could be mine
Onyore naranda buna murwa	So as to spread on it low growing grass
Otangori e'Manga ebe yane	I wish Manga could be mine
Onyore naranda buna murwa	So as to spread on it like low growing grass
Ee buna murwa, ee buna murwa	Like grass, ee like grass
Onyore naranda buna murwa	So as to spread on it like low growing grass
E buna murwa	Ee like grass
Onyore naranda buna murwa	So as to spread on it like low growing grass
E buna murwa	Ee like grass
Onyore naranda buna murwa---aa	So as to spread on it like low growing grass
Ee Onchari 'nkorere're -- ee	We the Bonchari people cry that
Otangori e'Manga ebe yane	Manga hill could be mine
Ee Onchari 'nkorere're -- ee	We the Bonchari people cry that
Otangori e'Manga ebe yane	Manga hill could be mine
Otangori e'Manga ebe yane	I wish Manga could be mine
Onyore naranda buna murwa--aaaa	So as to spread on it like low growing grass
Oraiyaa, oraiyaa,	Oraiyaa, oraiyaa,
Chingero bonyangero-ta!	Song of Songs-ta!

Chapter 10
Poetry of Historical Events, Immigration and Settlement

In this section we shall look at poetry that were sung years back and have a historical association. Most of these songs were sung to me by Dr. Evans Nyamwaka, a history lecturer at Kisii University. One other song was sung to me by Peter Nyamache Getenga and Dr. Matunda Nyanchama.

One of the songs Dr. Evans Nyamwaka sang to me, *Enchara Nembe*, draws us to the migration of the Abagusii. In their immigration, the Abagusii settled in Kisumu and, while there, they experienced a terrible famine. There was no food to eat. As a result of this, they moved to Kano where they could find food. It is at Kano where they sung the song "Enchara n'Embe" to remind them of the hard life they led while living in Kisumu.

Enchara Nembe	**Famine is Terrible**
Echara nembe yaitire Mogusii	Famine is terrible, it has stricken Mogusii
Baminto aaria Kisumo	Surely there at Kisumo
Yaitire Mogusii	It has stricken Mogusii
Torende endagera yaito	Let us take care of our food.
Baminto Mwamogusii.	All of us the Abagusi
Echara nembe yaitire Mogusii	Famine is terrible, it has stricken Mogusii
Baminto aaria Kisumo	Surely there at Kisumo
Yaitire Mogusii	It has stricken Mogusii
Torende endagera yaito	Let us take care of our food
Baminto Mwamogusii.	All of us the Abagusii

"Enchara Nembe" is an oral poem that is sung to date to encourage people to work hard and to preserve their foods.

Famine has always been a concern of Omogusii. Peter Nyamache Getenga recalls that in 1928 *chingige*, Locusts, invaded Gusii and devoured all green plants, including beans, maize, sorghum, millet, etc. There was solely nothing that remained for people to eat. People roasted and ate the locusts and many of them died out of diarhea. During these difficult times, the people composed and sung a song called "Enyangweso" (locusts). The word *Motoboro* comes from the word *Omotoboro* (unripe plant crop) or *ogotobora* (to harvest unripe plant crop for consumption because of the compulsion of hunger). *Enyangweso* is a word the people used to refer to *chingige* (locusts).

Enyangweso	**The Locust**
Ee enyangweso yarwa Bogere	Yes the locusts have invaded from Luoland
Eee Bogere	Yes Luo land
Enyangweso yarwa	The locusts have come
Ee enyangweso yarwa Bogere	Yes locusts have invaded from Luoland
Ee Bogere	Yes Luo land
Ee Bogere	Yes Luo land
Baba motoboro nyangweso	Baba, unripe crops eaten by locusts
Abamura 'bache barwane	Let young men come and fight them
Ee barwane	Yes fight them
Abamura bache	Let young men come
Ee abamura bache barwane	Let young men come and fight them
Ee ee barwane	Yes fight them
Ee barwane	Yes fight them
Baba motoboro nyangweso	Baba, unripe crops eaten by locusts

The song says that locusts have come from the bordering Luoland. It states that they have eaten unripe plant crops. The song calls upon young men to come and help stop the invasion of these locusts. Nyamache recalls that both men and women were involved in stopping these insects. When the locusts ate everything and nothing was left, the people now turned to the insects and made them food.

There is another version of this oral poem collected and sung by Matunda Nyanchama (12/01/2019).

Nyangweso

According to Matuda Nyanchama, the locusts invaded Gusii in the 1930s and destroyed every green plant in their way leaving a suffering population in its wake. Neither the grass nor the crops survived the invasion; not the trees nor cultivated plants survived. There was devastation. In the following oral poem, the singer laments what happened to his/her mother's crop the millet, wimbi, etc. starting by saying that an alarm has been raised down Manga Escarpment indicating a sign of danger.

Enyangweso	**Enyangweso[1]**
Ekebwe ngiakura Manga inse	A jackal has wailed down in the Manga Valley
Ee Manga inse ekebwe ngiakura	Yes, down the Manga Valley the jackal has wailed
Ekebwe ngiakura Manga inse	A jackal has wailed down in the Manga Valley
Ee Manga inse Baba omotengere Nyangweso	Yes, down Manga Valley; mother see what[2] Nyangweso[3] (locusts)[4] has done
Obori bwa baba ekeande	A jackal has wailed down in the Manga Valley
Ee ekeande obori bwa Baba	Yes, down the Manga Valley the jackal has wailed
Obori bwa baba ekeande	A jackal has wailed down in the Manga Valley
Ee ekeande Baba omotengere Nyangweso	Yes, down Manga Valley; mother see what[5] Nyangweso[6] (locusts)[7] has done
Ee Nyangweso yacha yaboria	Ee! Nyangweso has come and eaten it (the finger millet) up
Ee yaboria Nyangweso yacha	Ee! Nyangweso has come and eaten it (the finger millet) up
Ee Nyangweso yacha yaboria	Ee! It has come and consumed it up
Ee yaboria Baba omotengere Nyagweso	Ee! Nyangweso has come and eaten it up

---

1   Translated with input from Nemwel Atemba, author of *Abagusii Wisdom Revisited*, Nsemia Inc. 2011

2   Referring to the devastation caused by Nyangweso

3   Note that Nyangweso referred to locusts (*chingige*)

4   Could also mean: see (in wonderment) what Nyangweso has done!

5   Large and heathy sorghum seeds conjure up the feeling of several eyes staring at one!

6   Note that Nyangweso referred to locusts (chingige)

7   Could also mean: see (in wonderment) what Nyangweso has done!

Amaemba a Baba amatogoro	Ee! It has come and consumed it up, mother see what Nyangweso has done
Ee amatogoro amaemba a Baba	My mother's 'staring' sorghum
Amaemba a Baba amatogoro	Eh!, my mother's 'staring' sorghum
Ee amatogoro Baba omotongere Nyangweso	My mother's 'staring[5]' sorghum
Ee Nyangweso yacha yayaria	Ee! Nyangweso has come and eaten it (the millet) up
Ee yayaria Nyangweso yacha	Ee! Nyangweso has come and eaten it (the millet) up
Ee Nyangweso yacha yayaria	Ee! Nyangweso has come and eaten it up
Ee yayaria Baba omotengere Nyagweso	Ee! It has come and consumed it up, mother see what Nyangweso has done

Chapter 11
Poetry Sung During Work

As we saw earlier in the previous chapters, hard work, responsibility and social life was the philosophy of the Omogusii. We saw the oral poem, *Mogisangio Akoreke Ekee*, which encouraged young men to work hard to acquire wealth which in turn put them in good stead to marry and sire children whom in turn became protectors of the families.

Omogusii Omong'aini

Just like "Mogisangio Akoreke Ekee," this oral poem also carries the philosophy of the Omogusii: hard work, economy, generosity, and social belonging. In the first stanza we note that Omogusii is a wise and intelligent person. He works hard to consume but more so 'keeps' a part of what he collects or harvests. Second stanza states that this philosophy of economy has been there since our great grand fathers. The third stanza states that Omogusii is generous and keeps something (food) for those who are away in the forest hunting/searching.

Omogusii Omong'aini	Omogusii is a clever person
Omogusii omong'aini	Omogusii is a clever person
Ng'a aera era ogacha	He works hard and saves
Aera era ogocha	Works hard and saves
Narero akogacha	Even these days he saves
Omogusii omong'aini	Omogusii is a clever person
Ng'a aera era ogacha	He works hard and saves
Aera era ogocha	Works hard and saves
Narero akogacha	Even these days he saves
Korwa bakoro baito	Since our great grand parents
Ng'a aera era ogacha	He works hard and saves
Aera era ogacha	Works hard and saves
Narero akogacha	Even these days he works hard and saves

Gachera 'bainani	He saves for those who are away
Ng'a aera era ogacha	He works hard and saves
Aera era ogacha	Works hard and saves
Narero akogacha	Even these days he saves
Korwa nyomba chieito	Since our great grand parents
Ng'a aera era ogacha	He works hard and saves
Aera era ogacha	Works hard and saves
Na rero akogacha	Even these days he works hard and saves
Omogusii omong'aini	Omogusii is a clever person
Ng'a aera era ogacha	He works hard and saves
Aera era ogocha	Works hard and saves
Narero akogacha	Even these days he saves

(Evans Omosa Nyamwaka, 2017)

Omotienyi Noerete

One of the oral work poems, *Omotienyi N'oerete,* was sung by a blacksmith as he made spears, swords, arrows, leg-rings and jingles. He sung the song to inspire himself in his work by praising his work and tools, praise himself, relate his experiences and expectations or scorn those who feared the demanding work, tried to interfere or were not interested in blacksmithery. Praising his work and the expected benefits, a blacksmith would suddenly sing "Omotienyi N'oerete."

Omotienyi N'oerete	**The Month is over**
Omotienyi n'oerete	The *month* is over
Ng'a Nyangirisa o yaye	You my customer
Nyangirisa oyaye	You my customer, oh yes
Omotienyi n'oerete	The month is over
Ng'a Nyangirisa o yaye	You my customer, oh yes
Nyangirisa oyaye	You my customer, oh yes
Ng'a aye eng'eria	Give me my due
Nyangirisa o yaye	You customer, oh yes
Nyangirisa o yaye	You my customer, oh yes
Ng'a n'emeremo ngokora buya	That I am now working nicely,
Nyangirisa oyaye	My customer, oh yes
Nyangirisa oyaye	My customer, oh yes

(Evans Omosa Nyamwaka, 2017)

The song was also sung to educate people on the fairness of paying workers their dues in good time. Some employers, in particular, the White settlers, would delay their workers' salaries or even reduce the pay citing ineffective job performance as the reason for it. The employee thus laments that he did a good job hence the need to be paid his full amount at the appropriate time, end month.

Ninki Ekio Obwate?

Hunting missions in the Abagusii community was also grouped as part of work. Dr. Evans Omosa Nyamwaka states that after the hunters killed wild game for food they carried it home as they sung "Ninki Ekio Obwate," an oral poem that depicted victory and success in their hunting mission.

Ninki Ekio Obwate?	**What Are You Carrying?**
'Nki ekio obwate	What are you carrying?
'Nkagoye 'mbwate	I am carrying a prey
Otakong'a'ndome	Give me I bite
Ng'ende korisia	I go to graze cattle
O yaye o yaye	Oh yes! Oh yes!
'Nki ekio obwate	What are you carrying?
'Nkagoye 'mbwate	I am carrying a prey
Otakong'a 'ndome	Give me I bite
Ng'ende korisia	I go to graze cattle
O yaye o yaye	Oh yes! Oh yes!

(Evans Omosa Nyamwaka, 2017)

Mbono Tokare Gocha

The song "Mbono Tokare Gocha" imitates a lion. It is a reminder to Abagusii that they were once hunters. The word *sibuori* is derived from the Luo word *sibuor* meaning lion. As we saw earlier, a number of hero, victory and war songs of the Abagusii were borrowed from the Luo people. It is speculated that this happened as a result of the Luo supporting Abagusii in wars, such as the battle of Mogori (Saosao).

Mbono Tokare Gocha	**It is now we are coming, we the lions**
'Mbono tokare gocha sibuori Nyarimo Moo	It is now we are coming, we the lions - Moo
'Mbono tokare gocha sibuori Nyarimo Moo	It is now we are coming, we the lions - Moo
Twairanire twensi 'ntwe sibuori nyarimo Moo	We have all come back, we lions - Moo
'Mbono tokare gocha 'ntwe sibuori nyarimoo Moo	It is now we are coming, we the lions - Moo
Twensi twairanire sibouri Nyarimo Moo	We have all come we lions - Moo.
'Mbono tokare gocha sibuori Nyarimo Moo	It is now we are coming, we the lions - Moo
'Mbono tokare gocha sibuori Nyarimo Moo	It is now we are coming, we the lions - Moo
Twairanire twensi 'ntwe sibuori nyarimo Moo	We have all come back, we lions - Moo
'Mbono tokare gocha 'ntwe sibuori nyarimoo Moo	It is now we are coming, we the lions - Moo
Twensi twairanire sibuori Nyarimo Moo	We have all come we lions - Moo.

(Evans Omosa Nyamwaka, 2017)

Mosaiga Osiberie Ong'e

One of the most common poems sung with reference to work/chores is "Mosaiga Osiberie Ong'e." It was sung at the beer party. It condemned people who were lazy and did not work hard. The song told the community not to share their belongings with people who did not work hard and encouraged them to only share it with those who work hard.

Mosaiga Osiberie Ong'e	**Sip and Give it to me**
Omosaiga siberia ong'e	Sip and give it to me, friend
Osiberie ong'e	Sip and give it to me
Osiberie ong'e omosaiga	Sip and give it to me, friend
Ae, ae, omosaiga	Ae, ae, friend
Toa n'onde	Don't give it to another person
Toa monto okobayabaya	Who is a wanderer (lazy)
Ae, ae, omosaiga	Ae, ae, friend
Mbono 'ngocha	I have arrived
Mbono 'ngocha omosaiga	I have come, friend
Ae, ae, omosaiga	Ae, ae, friend

Kai barure	Where have they been?
Kai barure, omosaiga	Where've they come from?
Ae, ae, omosaiga	Ae, ae, friend
Barure bw' Okiango omoribo	They've come from Okiango's home
Ae, ae, omosaiga	Ae, ae, friend
Nao barure bw'Okiango Omorure	They've come from Okiango's home.

This oral poem was sung by old men usually during a function at home. They sang this song to show that they loved one another. It is addressing *omosaiga,* a friend/colleague. The singer tells his friend to sip beer that they are sharing and give the *ekee* (traditional plate made of reeds in which food and beer was served) back to him. He should not give it to someone else, especially one that is lazy. No one is allowed to share with the lazy ones. By leaving out the lazy ones, the latter will learn to work hard as it is a virtue in the Abagusii community.

Chapter 12
From Tradition to Modern: Poetry of Transition

This chapter contains oral poems composed and performed during the period between tradition and the coming of the white colonist. The compositions during that time show disillusionment and disgruntlement. The poetry seems to indicate a moment of confusion and not knowig what is right and wrong in the community. People had started adopting western mannerisms and styles of living. Things such as bicycles, wearing long trousers, and stone houses were new features in the land of Gusii.

Abamura ba Amakia Aya

This song, contributed and translated by Matunda Nyanchama, criticises modern young men for their lack of concern for wealth; wealth in traditional Gusii society meant livestock, usually cattle. The song goes on to show how young men, in olden times, used to be vigilant protecting their cattle from being stolen. They lived in military encampments where they watched for intruders; and if one did, an alarm was raised to pursue the raiders because the people could not fathom life without milk for their children. The song details how the thieves could be pursued and killed. Once that happened, then there was rejoicing by everyone.

Abamura ba Amakia Aya	**These (Modern) Days' Young Men)**
Abamura ba 'makia aya,	These days' young men
Abamura ba amakia aya,	These days' young men
Abamura ba amakia aya,	These days' young men
Abamura ba 'makia aya,	These days' young men
Abamura ba amakia aya,	These days' young men
Abamura ba amakia aya,	These days' young men

Tibari korenda enibo,	They don't care of wealth,
'Mbari korenda enibo buna baria bakare	they don't care for wealth like their predecessors
Tibari korenda enibo,	They don't care of wealth,
'Mbari korenda enibo buna baria bakare	they don't care of wealth like their predecessors
Bare korenda enibo	Who used to care of wealth
Bare korenda enibo ase ebisarate biabo	Who used to care of wealth in their military encampments
Bare korenda enibo	Who used to care of wealth
Bare korenda enibo ase ebisarate biabo	Who used to care for wealth in their military encampments
Omoibi ogochia gocha	If a thief came,
Omoibi ogochia gocha erio rende bakura	If a thief came, when a thief came they raised an alarm
Omoibi ogochia gocha	If a thief came,
Omoibi ogochia gocha erio rende bakura	If a thief came, when a thief came they raised an alarm
Erio rende bakura	Then they raise an alarm
Erio rende bakura erio rende bakura	Then they raise an alarm, then they raise an alarm, then they raise an alarm
Erio rende bakura	Then they raise an alarm
Erio rende bakura erio rende bakura	Then they raise an alarm, then they raise an alarm, then they raise an alarm
Ooo yaye kura monoooo	Oooyaye raise the alarm higher
Yaye kura mono	Oooyaye raise the alarm higher
Nyang'era[1] yaito yarimeire Sigisi	Our Nyang'era has disappeared to Kipsigis land
Abana baito ninki barache koria?	What will our children eat?
Nyang'era yaito yarimeire Sigisi	Our Nyang'era[1] has disappeared to Kipsigis land
Abana baito ninki barache koria?	What will our children eat?

---

1   This is the name of a pitch black cow.

Omoibi ogochia gocha	If a thief came,
Omoibi ogochia gocha obetirwe ritimo	If a thief came, when a thief came he is promptly speared
Omoibi ogochia gocha	If a thief came,
Omoibi ogochia gocha obetirwe ritimo	If a thief came, when a thief came he is promptly speared
Erio rende bakura	Then they rejoice,
Erio rende bachenga/batenga erio rende bachenga	Then they rejoice, then they rejoice, then they rejoice
Erio rende bakura	Then they rejoice,
Erio rende bachenga/batenga	Then they rejoice, then they rejoice, then they rejoice
erio rende bachenga	Then they rejoice,
Kurera abanto	Tell everyone and all
Chiombe chiairanire	Our cattle have been returned
Kurera abanto	Tell everyone and all
Chiombe chiairanire	Our cattle have been returned
Korua Sigisi; Korua Sigisi Rogoro Sigisi	From the land of the Kipsigis, from the land of the Kipsigis, up from the land of the Kipsigis

Otiso Okare o'Monyange

This song, sang perhaps before 1920 or even early 1920s was contributed by Matunda Nyanchama. He explains that marriage was a major milestone in traditional Gusii community. When young men became of age, they were expected to marry and settle to raise a family. However, as things changed, one Otiso o'Monyange acted in the contrary. It was the time when a few (very few) people wore trousers or rode bicycles. Otiso was ridiculed for choosing to buy a pair of long trousers and a bike prior to getting married. The singer wonders whether these items would serve the role of a wife: fetch firewood and light a fire; fetch water and cook! The refrain "one, two, three, four" indicates that some English words had started making it into Ekegusii

Otiso Okare o'Monyange	**Otiso the Son of Monyange**
Otiso akagora enyange ee	Otiso bought a bicycle, yes

Otiso akagora enyange ee,	Otiso bought a bicycle, yes
Akagora enyange ataranyoma	He bought a bicycle before marrying
E! n'Otiso okare o'Monyange.	E! Otiso the son Monyange
Aaee E! n'Otiso okare o'Monyange eh!I	Aaee Otiso the son of Monyange eh!
Iye! Iye! Iye! n'Otiso okare o'Monyange one, two, three four	Iye! Iye! Iye! Otiso the son of Monyange
Akagora erong'i ataranywoma!	He bought long trousers before marrying
Aaee E! Akagora erong'i ataranywoma eh!	Aaee he bought long trousers before marrying
Iye! Iye! Iye! Akagora erong'i ataranywoma one, two, three four	Iye! Iye! Iye! He bought long trousers before marrying
Erong'i nero erachie roche?Aaee E!	Will the trousers fetch water?
Erong'i nero erachie roche?eh!	Aaee E! Will the trousers fetch water?

The following is another version of the above song provided by Jane Marando Obuchi

Otiso Okare O'Manyange	**Otiso Son of Manyange**
Otiso okare Omanyange, ee	Yes, Otiso, son of Manyange
Otiso okare Omanyange, ee	Yes, Otiso, son of Manyange
Ee Otiso akagora enyange	Yes, Otiso, son of Manyange
One, two, three, four, eswa, swaswa	One, two, three, four, sure, sure, sure
Akagora enyange ataranyuoma, ee	He bought a bicycle before getting married, yes
Akagora enyange ataranyuoma, ee	He bought a bicycle before getting married, yes
Ee, akagora enyange ataranyuoma	Yes, yes, he bought a bicycle before getting married,
One, two, three, four, eswa, swaswa	one two, three, four, sure, sure, sure
Enyange nero agotoma roche, ee	Will he send the bicycle to the river, yes?
Enyange nero agotoma roche, ee	Will he send the bicycle to the river, yes?
Ee, wnyange nero agotoma roche	Yes, yes, the bicycle is what he sends to the river
One, two, three, four, eswa, swaswa	One, two, three, four, sure, sure, sure

Enyange n'ero agotoma kwaa, ee	Will he send bicycle to bring vegetables, yes?
Enyange n'ero agotoma kwaa, ee	Will he send bicycle to bring vegetables, yes?
Ee, Enyange n'ero agotoma kwaa	Yes, yes, the bicycle is what he sends to bring vegetables
One, two, three, four, eswa, swaswa	One, two, three, four, sure, sure, sure
Enyange nero agotoma etinga, ee	Will he send bicycle to the posho mill, yes?
Enyange nero agotoma etinga, ee	Will he send bicycle to the posho mill, yes?
Ee, Enyange nero agotoma etinga	Yes, yes, the bicycle is what he sends to the posho mill
One, two, three, four, eswa, swaswa	One, two, three, four, sure, sure, sure
Otiso omoriri kware, ee	Otiso you were stupid, yes
Otiso omoriri kware, ee	Otiso you were stupid, yes
Ee, Otiso omoriri kware	Yes, Otiso you were stupid
One, two, three, four, eswa, swaswa	One, two, three, four, sure, sure, sure

(Obuchi:43-44: 2019)

A bicycle *(enyange)* was an asset that could only be owned by the well-to-do in society. These included the teachers. Anybody who owned a bicycle was held in very high esteem by the community members. Otiso would not receive such honour due to the fact that he was not married.

Chiama Roche

This oral poem also must have been sung during the transition from tradition to modern. Like the above oral piece that condemned Otiso o'Monyange for buying a long trouser, this one condemns the wearing of long trousers by girls.

Chiama Roche	**Growing in the River**
Chiama roche	Growing in the river
Chiama roche	Growing in the river
Chiama roche	Growing in the river
Chiama roche	Growing in the river

Seito chinchugu chiama roche chiama roche	At our home groundnuts grow in the river
Seito chinchugu chiama roche chiama roche	At our home groundnuts grow in the river
Okorina irongo	Climbing up the loft
Okorina irongo	Climbing up the loft
Okorina irongo	Climbing up the loft
Okorina irongo	Climbing up the loft
Seito 'momura mokayayu okorina irongo	A badly-mannered boy who climbs up the loft
Seito 'momura mokayayu okorina irongo	A badly-mannered boy who climbs up the loft
Okobeka eberi okobeka eberi	Wearing a long trouser
Okobeka eberi okobeka eberi	Wearing a long trouser
Seito 'moiseke mokayayu okobeka eberi	A badly-mannered girl who wears a long trouser
Seito 'moiseke mokayayu okobeka eberi	A badly-mannered girl who wears a long trouser

New Political Order–Kare Kare Kare

This was sung in the 1950s and at the height of the struggle for independence. It speaks of Jomo Kenyatta and how, prior to his birth, his parents wished for him to be born. It speaks of the same for Lawrence Sagini, and how a long, long time ago his parents wished to have him born. It praises the people of Kitutu for having borne Sagini, the son of Ndemo, who has joined the Legislative Council (LEGCO). (NB: the LEGCO was more like parliament in the colonial days; for the first time in the late 1940s the colonial government started appointing Africans as member of LEGCO and Lawrence Sagini was one of them.

Kare Kare Kare	**A long, Long Time Ago**
Kare kare kare Kenyatta ataraiborwa	A long, long time ago before Kenyatta was born
Kare kare kare Kenyatta ataraiborwa	A long, long time ago before Kenyatta was born
Ng'ina na ise ebare korera 'nKenyatta totagete	His mother and father used to cry that Kenyatta be born

Ng'ina na ise ebare korera 'nKenyatta totagete	His mother and father used to cry that Kenyatta be born
Kare kare kare Sagini ataraiborwa	A long, long time ago before Sagini was born
Kare kare kare Sagini ataraiborwa	A long, long time ago before Sagini was born
Ng'ina na ise ebare korera 'nSagini totagete	His mother and father used to cry that Sagini be born
Ng'ina na ise ebare korera 'nSagini totagete	His mother and father used to cry that Sagini be born
Ense eye yaito ''mBogetutu togotogia	In our part of the world we praise the land of Kitutu
Ense eye yaito ''mBogetutu togotogia	In our part of the world we praise the land of Kitutu
Bwaiboire omwana ore o'Ndemo Sagini Ochire Legco	You have borne Ndemo's son, Sagini has gone to the Legco
Bwaiboire omwana ore o'Ndemo Sagini Ochire Legco	You have borne Ndemo's son, Sagini has gone to the Legco

Tiga Mbori Nyairabu

Nyairabu was the son of Mogendi (Ogoso) in Tabaka region of Gusii. It is said that Nyairabu was the first one to be employed by a white colonialist. His work was to count the Abakuria and the Abagusii. He was the first born. Nyairabu's father, Ogoso, had married Ogoso's mother at old age. Because the old man had 'finished' bearing children with his other wives, he decided to call his son *omokogoti bosaigo* (just the last born). This was because, although the boy was a first born to the man's youngest wife, he had finished bearing children.

Ogoso is referred to as Nyakurukumba because he and his mother wandered across Luoland. His father had died while Ogoso was about 26 years old. He is referred to as "*n'eyang'ina akwambara/agotwara* to indicate that he lives at his mother's place. His father's place was not known (probably it was at Kitutu). It is believed that the descendants of Ogoso are found in Luoland, especially in Sakwa and Makalda mines.

Oral Poetry in Africa

| **Tiga Mbori Nyairabu** | **Let Me Ask Nyairabu** |

Ee tiga 'mborie Nyairabu Ee let me ask Nyairabu
Ee tiga 'mborie Nyairabu-uuuu Ee let me ask Nyairabu

Ee tiga 'mborie Nyairabu Ee let me ask Nyairabu
Ee tiga 'mborie Nyairabu Ee let me ask Nyairabu
Nyairabu ore o'Mogendi--aaaa Nyairabu at Mogendi's --aaa

Ee tiga 'mborie Nyairabu Ee let me ask Nyairabu
Ee tiga 'mborie Nyairabu-uuuu Ee let me ask Nyairabu

Ee tiga 'mborie Nyairabu Ee let me ask Nyairabu
Ee tiga 'mborie Nyairabu Ee let me ask Nyairabu
Nyairabu ore o'Mogendi--aaaa Nyairabu at Mogendi's--aaa

Ee Nyairabu ore o'Mogendi--aaa Ee Nyairabu at Mogendi's--aaa
Nyanamba chire kuaa-aaaa With a badge on the chest—aaa

Ee omokogoti bosaigo—aaa Ee, just a last-born--aa
Omokogoti bw'Ogoso—aaaa Last born of Ogoso—aaa

Ogoso Nyakurukumba--aaa Ogoso, the wanderer--aaa
N'eyang'ina akwambara--aaa Who lives with his mother--aaa
Ee n'eyang'ina agotwara--aaa Who lives at her mother's place--aaa

Nyarinda O'Sugutaire

This oral poem speaks of Nyarinda, the first Kisii woman to be married to a European. Having been married outside Abagusii community, the song views her as loose and immoral. To be a 'loiterer' refers to the act of wandering or seeking or soliciting, or simply practising prostitution.

The white man to whom she is married, is called Anderson (Anda, as the local people pronounced his name). He, like other white people, has built his house in the "bush." The bush here refers to the lush or green fence that surrounds his permanent house.

This song was sung with an accompaniment of percussion instruments, such as *chindege* or *chinchigiri*, or *ekerandi*

Nyarinda O'Sugutaire	**Nyarinda is Loitering**
Nyarinda o'sugutaire, Nyarinda o'sugutaire!	Nyarinda is loitering, Nyarinda is loitering!
Nyarinda o'sugutaire, Nyarinda o'sugutaire!	Nyarinda is loitering, Nyarinda is loitering!
Baba o'minto Nyarinda o'sugutaire, Nyarinda o'sugutaire!	Oh My, Nyarinda is loitering, loitering, Nyarinda's loitering
Baba o'minto Nyarinda o'sugutaire, Nyarinda O'sugutaire	Oh My, Nyarinda is loitering, loitering, Nyarinda's loitering
Ase enchera ekogenda, ase enchera ekogenda!	Where the road leads, where the road leads
Ase enchera ekogenda, ase enchera ekogenda!	Where the road leads, where the road leads
Baba o'minto ase enchera ekogenda, ase enchera ekogenda!	Oh my, where the road leads, where the road leads
Baba o'minto ase enchera ekogenda, ase enchera ekogenda!	Oh my, where the road leads, where the road leads
Omosongo Bwana Anda (Anderson) bw'agachire rigena rinani ime!	A white man, Mr. Anderson, has built a stone house in the bush
Omosongo Bwana Anda (Anderson) bw'agachire rigena rinani ime!	A white man, Mr. Anderson, has built a stone house in the bush
Baba o'minto	
Omosongo Bwana Anda (Anderson) bw'agachire rigena rinani ime!	A white man, Mr. Anderson, has built a stone house in the bush
Baba o'minto	
Omosongo Bwana Anda (Anderson) bw'agachire rigena rinani ime!	A white man, Mr. Anderson, has built a stone house in the bush

Nyaboke Nagokania

During the second world war many Gusii young men were captured and taken to fight in Alexandria, Egypt, Japan, Pama and South Africa. When these youg men came back after the war, many of them had contracted gonorrhea and syphills, diseases that were not known in Gusii. They infected young ladies in Gusii. This oral poem was sung in 1940s after the war and cautions a young lady called Nyaboke against falling in love with an ex-soldier who might be infected. The poem was sung to me by John S. Akama in 2019.

Nyaboke Nagokania		**Nyaboke You were Cautioned**
Nyaboke nagokania		Nyaboke you were cautioned
Nyaboke nagokania		Nyaboke you were cautioned
'Momura o'militari		Do not fall in love with an ex-soldier
'Momura o'militari		Do not fall in love with an ex-soldier
Omomura o'militari n'oborwaire	*konare*	He has a veneral disease
Omomura o'militari n'oborwaire	*konare*	He has a veneral disease
Konare n'oborwaire Tisababa	*arusetie*	He contracted while in Addis Ababa
Konare n'oborwaire Tisababa	*arusetie*	He contracted while in Addis Ababa
Nare n'oborwaire Tisababa	*arusetie*	He contracted while in Addis Ababa
Nare n'oborwaire Tisababa	*arusetie*	He contracted while in Addis Ababa
Ae omoyo		Ae, we love you
Ae omoyo		Ae, we love you

Summary, Conclusion & Recommendations

The Gusii oral poetry, as has been realized, cannot be complete without the performance of the same. It is poetry dead on the page unless performed with an accompaniment of instruments such as obokano, chindege, chinchigiri and ekeng'iring'iri. As Finnegan (1976) postulates, "oral literature depends on a performer who formulates it in words on a specific occasion--there is no other way in which it can be realized as a literary product."(2). This book has only documented the oral poems in their written form. A study need to be done to capture the performative aspect of these poems. This is because in its formative form, the poetry will reveal the reaction and role of the audience, the accompanying instruments, and the noise and sounds – as all these contribute towards the production of meaning in oral poetry.

Oral poetry in Gusii community fall into two types: the general oral poetry and *emeino* (classical poetry). While the former is elastic and can be elongated and shortened, the latter is fixed and cannot be changed. The latter has to be sung the way they were originally composed. However, you realize from the book that while the general oral poetry we have analysed come from all locations in Gusii, the classical poems only come from Bogirango and Machoge. *Emeino* from Kitutu and Nyaribari need to be researched and analyzed as we feel that these ones have been left out in this book.

This book covers and analyses a good number of children's oral poems. It is noted that children in the Abagusii community, presented their oral poetry as play-songs or singing games in which they made movements, danced, sung and made patterns using their hands, bodies and legs. It was discovered that Abagusii children play-songs utilized words and expressions that did not necessarily have meaning. Words such as *oombe* (refer to the earlier explanation on the corrupted form of this song...*Oombe*...Oh baby!) in "Omwana

Arare" and *kambusi karangera* in the play song "Kambusi Karangera" do not have any particular meaning. They were either borrowed by children from neighbouring communities, or were coined to create the desired rhythm or play patterns. Other words were just coined to help with tongue-twisting and enhance speech and skills in expressing oneself. It was concluded that the singing games provided pleasure and entertainment to children as well as provided a platform on which the children were largely socialized.

The book covers oral poetry sung during female and male circumcision. It was discovered that circumcision practised as a rite of passage. Most oral pieces for circumcision were heavily loaded with symbolism and indirect language. This is because the poems comprise of *amang'ana ansoni,* taboo words.

It was noted that the oral poetry sung during circumcision was obscene and utilised *amang'ana a'nsoni* (taboo words). It was concluded that this indecency was meant to help people to 'unwind'. People, having done work throughout the year, been descent all along and occupied themselves with building the community, they needed a moment of rest and a moment of 'bursting out', in which they threw all cares to the air. It was an occasion in which they reflected back to the years of hard work, a future that was ahead and how to bring fulfillment to life. They had to 'unwind', 'exhale' and 'let it go' after a whole year of involvement and occupation, after a period of carefully behaving well, avoiding taboo words and actions.

Oral poetry for marriage indicated tension and anxiety among nubile boys and girls. The society looked forward to see them marry and have children; this exerted a lot pressure upon them. The acquisition of dowry to enable a boy to marry was a big challenge. Impotence was despised and any boy or girl who delayed his/her marriage found it difficult to live among the members of the community. Most oral poems for marriage were wrapped in symbolisms to avoid direct language.

The book also features oral poems for married people. It was discovered that most poetry attempt to address women about the importance of men in their lives, while admonishing woman who did not behave well. The poetry in this section places women in low cadre compared to men.

Poetry of old age comes out as a form of lamentation. The poems show old men and women regretting about their old age, and wishing they were young again. They recall when they were young they had all the energy to do all types of activities.

This book covers massive poetry of inter-clan and inter-ethnic skirmishes and war. It was concluded that a lot of these violence was orchestrated by cattle rustling. In those days animals were a form of wealth and were used in batter-trading. This importance attached to them tempted young men to go out to fight and steal cattle. Abagusii fought among themselves but also fought neighbouring tribes such as the Maasais and the Kalenjins.

The book highlights poetry on historical events, immigration and settlement. From the oral poems one can tell the journey of the Omogusii from Misiri (Egpt) to his present day home. The oral compositions tell the challenges they encountered on their immigration and places they settled at different times in their journey.

Oral poetry of work, indicates that Omogusii was an intelligent person. He embraced hard work but also encouraged saving for future use. As the oral poem, "Mosaiga Osiberie Ong'e" states, Gusii community discouraged laziness and people who wanted to get free things they had not worked for. The oral piece, "Mogisankio Akoreke Ekee" summarizes the philosophy of the Omogusii about hard work.

Gusii community did not remain pure and clean as it was. It was invaded by the colonialist. Young men were captured during the second world war to fight in Pama, Alexandria, Japan, etc. New commodities, new ways of living were imported to the community. The book has captured this new phenomenon as a transition from tradition to modern life.

Glossary of Terms

Ekegusii Word	Meaning
Abagirango	Descendants of one of the Mogusii's children
Abagusii	The people who live in Gusii
Abamura	Circumcised boys
Abaisia	Uncircumcised lads
amang'ana ansoni	Taboo words
Borangi	One of the clans in Gusii. Abarangi (Orangi) are the people who live in Borangi
Bogirango	One of the Gusii clans. Abagirango (ogirango) are the people of Bogirango clan
Botabori	One of the Gusii clan. Omotabori (Otabori) is a member of that clan
Chinchigiri	Small pieces of metal used as a musical instruments
Chindege	A cymbal made of metals that is tied to an animal's neck to alert the owner of its whereabouts
Ching'aya	These are bigger shields that are meant for the whole body made from cow-hide. Unlike *chinguba, they* are bigger in size. (Singular, *Eng'aya*)
Chinguba	cow-hide made shields (Singular *Enguba*)
Ebiige	Mat made of straw used as a door
Egesibi	A tiny, 'mischevious' bird that used tobe found in Gusii; seen as cheeky and cunning.
Egesicho	This was a small piece of cloth the men hang round their hips and covered only the front part of their private parts, leaving the bottoms bare.
Ekee	
Ekerandi	Gourd
Ekiige	(Plural. Ebiige)
Eng'aya	
Engoba	Hide used as clothe in the olden times
Oraiyaa	This is a praise name
Esigani	The go-between in the Abagusii community between a bride and groom during courtship

Etago	This was made from a certain soil and milk ghees and applied by young men on their skins
Gusii	The land on which Abagusii tribe live
Kerario	Refers to the spot in the field on which the cows are tethered.
Korera	The mother and/or father to a man who has married your daughter
Mbisiringi	a type of tree in Gusii that sheds leaves and grows some more leaves
Mogusii	Ancestors of the Abagusii
Obokano	the Abagusii eight-string instrument
Omogumo	A type of tree growing in Gusii
Omwobo	A type of tree that grows in Gusii land. (Plural emiobo)
Oraiyaa	This is a name to praise someone
Orochoa	This is a field with green grass that bears seeds.
orotuba.	Circumciser's trough
Siomia	To peep
Shukas	The traditional attires won by the Maasai tribe bordering Abagusii.
Sumi	The first room of traditional Kisii hut.

References

Abai, Ochoi (2015). *The History and Traditions of Abagusii of Kenya: Mwanyagetinge:* Printed in the USA, Metrographics

Akama, S.J.(2017) *The Gusii of Kenya: Social, Economic, Cultural, Political and Judicial Perspective*: Nairobi: Nsemia Inc. Publishers

_____ (2018) *The Untold Story: Gusii Survival Techniques and Resistance to the Establishment of British Colonial Rule:* Nairobi: Nsemia Inc. Publishers

Finnegan, R. (1976). *Oral Literature in Africa,* Nairobi Kenya, Oxford University Press.

Kihara, C. P. (2013).On mchongoano and riddles in Kenya: *The Journal of Pan African Studies,* vol.6, no.6, December 2013

Kihara, C.P .&Schröder, H. (2012).A relevance-theoretical analysis of aspects of **mchongoano.** *The University of Nairobi Journal of Language and Linguistics, Vol. 2 (2012),* 63-78

Ngugi, P. (2010). Nafasi na ubunifu katika mchezo wa watoto wa "mchongoano", katikaP.S. Malangwa and L.H. Bakize (ed) *Kioo cha lugha, journal of the institute ofKiswahili studies,* Dar es Salaam.VOL 8. 2010. 67 – 79. ISSN 0856552 X

Obuchi, J.M (2019) Chingero Chi'Abagusii, Chaphil, Eldoret

Okemwa, Christopher (2011) *Riddles of the Abagusii of Kenya: Gems of Wisdom from the African Continent.* Ontario: Nsemia Inc. Publishers

_____(2012) *Proverbs of Abagusii of Kenya: Meaning and Aplication.* Ontario: Nsemia Inc. Publishers

Orina, Felix (2014). Analysis of Symbolism and Transience in the Oral Literature of Abagusii of Western Kenya.Ph.D Thesis. Nairobi: University of Nairobi (Unpublished).

Nyang'era, Nelson K. (1999) *The Making of Man and Woman Under Abagusii Customary Laws.*Kisii: Dal-Rich Printers

www.ingramcontent.com/pod-product-compliance
Lightning Source LLC
Chambersburg PA
CBHW022022220426
43663CB00007B/1179